MW01244516

RUNGS ON MY LADDER

A Compelling Memoir of Faith

Foreword by Candi Staton

Rungs on my Ladder

Eleanor Riley

ISBN 978-1-882185-90-0

Library of Congress Control Number: 2006936687

All scripture references are taken from the Holy Bible, King James Version. Used by permission.

Contact the author at:
Email: Erileystbk@aol.com

Published by Cornerstone Publishing
Philadelphia, Pennsylvania
www.cornerstonepublishing.com

Cover design by Precision Imaging Designs.
Printed in Canada.

Eleanor Riley

RUNGS ON MY LADDER

A Compelling Memoir of Faith

Foreword by Candi Staton

*T*o my precious family,

my husband, Cecil Riley,

and

my daughters, Elizabeth and Esther Riley.

ACKNOWLEDGMENTS

I must first acknowledge the Ruler of my life, who watches over me, protecting me from harm, and has guided me through this book: God the Father, God the Son, and God the Holy Spirit. Thanks to Him for wisdom, knowledge, and understanding.

To my friend for life, Minister Candi Staton, who wrote the Foreword, I thank you so very much. May God continue His blessings on your life and ministry.

To my precious husband, Cecil, thanks for putting up with me sneaking into bed at two and three o'clock almost every morning, especially during my final draft.

Elizabeth and Esther, I thank and love you both for your love and support as always, even in choosing the picture for the cover. May the blessings of God follow you all the days of your lives.

I especially thank you, Monodel Oliverre, for your help towards the end of my draft, when it seemed I would not make the deadline. I appreciate your help and support.

Thanks to Rosie Edwards-Brown for your contribution towards my final chapters. I especially looked forward to your instant messages on late nights asking if I was okay. I love you.

Thanks also to my sister, Caulette, for your special note about the author. I love you.

This acknowledgment would not be complete without thanking Evangelist Vera Paul and Pastor Madge Boyd for confirming the Lord's instructions to write my autobiography. This was just two days apart from the prophetic word of the Lord.

Best of all, to my very good friend "Stitchie," you have been a tower of strength to me. For your help in accomplishing this goal, for all the information, the interest and prayers. Thanks so much. I love you.

To the staff of Cornerstone Publishing, especially Autumn Cherry, for believing in my life's story and giving me the opportunity to publish it. Thank you for helping to make this project become a reality.

Special thanks to William Greenleaf of Port Angeles, WA, for his final editorial touches to *Rungs on my Ladder*. For this I am so grateful.

CONTENTS

CONGRATULATIONS

*C*ongratulations are in order, Eleanor, for your steadfast faith and unwavering courage to always have the fortitude to take that daring plunge into whatever you desire.

As your husband, I have had the privilege of sharing more than half of your life with you and have known you better than anyone else. The details of your autobiography will certainly help to map out the way for our children, and all those who read your faith's journey.

Thank you for your constant commitment to truth, holding onto God's unchanging hand with the understanding and sound belief that He never fails.

I pray that this book will be read far and wide, and that it will suffer only from years of use.

This will be a reference always in our lives, only to remind us of our blessings — to name them one by one.

Congratulations again for this legacy of love, peace, and joy. I am blessed to have you as my wife.

- Cecil

PREFACE

*T*he time has come to share the special contents of this book with someone whose life may desire quiet times in order to gain some inner strength to deal with situations that are hostile and may seem hopeless. Realization faces us now, as it is written for him who must *"read while he runs."* This book is written for you to secure the inner fortitude to stand against the wiles of the devil. When he comes in like a flood and amidst the swirling currents, God will give you added strength and renewed life in Him.

We have to deal with the limits of time because we are not yet in eternity, whether or not we want to acknowledge that the end is near. This is what jolts me to write the autobiography of Eleanor Ridgeway-Riley. It will reveal who I really am and where I came from before time changes to eternity.

A ladder is used for either ascending or descending, whichever way it necessitates. As we have often heard: *"The sky is the limit!"* It does not matter how high each rung, God will lift us up. Sometimes our rungs become worn because they have been used so much. Today, we are at the top; tomorrow we may be at the bottom. God does not repair the rungs; He replaces them. In His wise supremacy, He knows they will be used again.

Many times we are not forgetting the things that are behind, but when we look back, it causes us to lose momentum and plummets us to the bottom of the ladder. He is not pointing us to heights, but He is leading us.

> *He leadeth me, He leadeth me,*
> *By His own hands He leadeth me.*
> *His faithful follower I would be,*
> *For by His hands He leadeth me.*

By sharing my life with others, I pray that it will cause someone to search within, for this will definitely lead to spiritual progress and stability. These experiences should only be a stepping stone to a more meaningful and infinite relationship with your Creator, the Almighty God.

As life goes on, I have realized that nothing good comes easily unless we press. Climbing is never the easiest job in the world. But if we surmise that there is something at the top worthwhile, then nothing will deter us from reaching there, even if it hurts in the process.

Let us remember, we are not asking for alms at the back entrance of life's kitchen, or for the crumbs that will satisfy us temporarily. We are the recipients of a never-ending treasury of riches, which money and strength in this world cannot wrestle from us.

When you settle down to read this book, do it with a cup of your favorite tea. As a matter of fact, make me a cup, too, please; no sugar. Remember, it is up to you to decide which way you want to go.

- Eleanor Riley

A SPECIAL NOTE

*Y*ou did it, Eleanor! Your trust in the Lord and hope for your true heart's desire has given you the privilege to dream big and create that which you hoped for. This is the evidence. This is your hope.

You are a wonderful sister who has led by example to know God and to know how mighty He is. Our mother had nine children, seven girls and two boys. As the oldest sister, you have given us an example to follow. We respect you, not just for being the oldest, but for being a sister who, no matter what, a phone call away is never a busy signal.

Growing up together, all of us have established our own personal relationships and not felt any distance that keeps us from sharing our life travels. That is a blessing.

Eleanor, you have always been the sister we looked to for strength and an uplifting word. You carry with you a love for family and sharing childhood moments of reciting poems by Louise Bennett. These moments in life are what we can look back on and remember with a smile.

Thanks, Eleanor, for all your love and love to our mother. May this book display a proud moment in your life, and may God put His blessing on it.

Love,

Your sister, Caulette

FORELJORD

*M*y friend, Eleanor Riley—

I first met her at a Caribbean festival in New York. We met again in Jamaica at a concert in Montego Bay. The concert left a lot to be desired, but there was one good thing that came out of it. I met a friend, Eleanor.

I've learned that people are a mystery until you know their history. Eleanor has conquered many of life's battles and is still standing to tell about it.

Rungs on my Ladder is a soul-stirring autobiography of a young woman who had a horrific life-changing experience—something that would have made many of us just fold up and give up. No, not Eleanor. She had an unwritten song to share with the world, and by the help and grace of God she has done just that. Hers is a story of pain, struggles, trials, and triumph. It just goes to show that, as one of my songs says, "God can make something out of nothing." He is a God who will never leave nor forsake you, an ever-present help in times of trouble.

Like Eleanor, let's keep on climbing that ladder—so that one day we will get to the last rung, and we will meet our Lord and Savior Jesus Christ, and He will say, "Welcome home, child. Well done."

- Minister Candi Staton
Stone Mountain, Georgia

TESTIMONIAL

*E*leanor Riley's beautiful and inspirational autobiography, *Rungs on my Ladder*, is a compelling tale of faith. Riley has combined the many challenges she has confronted in life with appropriately selected passages from the Bible to illustrate the message that our Lord has for us, His children, if only we would take heed and believe that with Him all things are possible.

In particular, she recounts how at an early age she found the Lord and never looked back, despite the devil's attempts to lead her astray. The Lord kept on lifting her higher and higher, and, with the use of each rung on her ladder, the Lord would replace it, not repair it, recognizing that the rungs may have to be used again with every new challenge as she moved up in faith.

Not only is this book a must-read for all Christians regardless of persuasion, but it is for all those who seek to lead in the Christian faith, as well.

Riley is pointed in her attack on those in the various Christian ministries who are but sheep in wolves' clothing. There are several disturbing and provocative accounts of those who could easily be described as hypocrites who have preyed on the innocent and unsuspecting.

Readers will undoubtedly enjoy this autobiography of a rural Jamaican girl with simple and modest beginnings in life, as well as appreciate her courage, determination, and daring in her quest to serve our Lord with malice towards none, despite the many adversities she had to overcome throughout her fascinating life.

Sister Riley's success in spreading the Word of the Lord via her successful music ministry is yet another amazing chapter in her life of faith.

In summary, readers will be truly inspired by this autobiography.

- Colonel Allan G. Douglas
Company Director

Chapter 1

THE BEGINNINGS

Rung 1: The Beginnings

*I*n order to help people remember the district where I am from, the phrase often used is, "In the west there is more land." I was born in a remote and quiet district named Peter's Vale in Westmoreland, Jamaica, in the West Indies – not to be confused with Peter's Field, as some sternly inform me.

In my culture, it is a common practice for babies to be registered not by their biological parents, but by a neighbor or a distant family member who quite likely is visiting at the time of birth. This is what happened at my birth, and I later had to correct an error made in the registering of my birth date. My registered name is Eleanor, but of course I was given an alias for easy memory.

One of my earliest memories is of my first day at school. It was a very rainy morning, as I recall. My mother had decided to enroll me in the May Pen Infant School. I remember crying all day for Mommy until it was time for dismissal. Eventually, I became familiar with the other children and began participating in the class activities. As I grew older and realized that school was inevitable, I began to gather as much knowledge as I possibly could on my own. It is said:

Labour for learning before you grow old
For learning is better than silver or gold.
Silver and gold will vanish away
But a good education will never decay.

With this in mind, I strove to become all that I could be. With the skillful help of my parents, teachers, and outstanding community leaders, I received the education that I needed to successfully take me to the next level of learning.

As a youth, I attended Sunday school at the Church of the First Born in May Pen. This is where I received in-depth teachings of the Holy Scriptures and an understanding of what the Word of God meant, as well as its capabilities in the life of a little girl. Even though I did not fully understand what my spiritual calling was at an early age, I could always sense God's infinite presence with me. One day, he allowed me to attend an old-fashioned revival meeting. I cannot tell you where, when, or how, but I knew the moment when He had spoken to me. I got up from my seat and the Holy Spirit led me to the altar. I must have been led by the Holy Spirit because I cannot remember how I got there. Through my tears, I asked Jesus into my heart. By the end of the meeting, I knew I was a changed child.

I began reading the Bible every day and learning the words of various songs until I was able to sing them on my own. Then, in a unique way, the Spirit of God began to reach others through me in songs, prayers, and demonstrations of His power. The first time that I encountered the Holy Spirit was when I was attending high school. One Monday evening, I came home from my classes and there was a woman waiting to accompany me. I was going to a house in the community where a young girl named Winnie lived. She was a member of our church who had become very ill. Upon entering the house, I was told that Winnie's sickness *was unto death.* She was at the point where she could not speak and she could barely do sign language.

As I walked into the room, I could see her lying on the bed. I looked around at the people standing there, and with all the strength and authority Christ had vested in me, I said, "If any of you standing here do not believe that Jesus Christ can heal this woman, please leave the room!" Most of the people left, and I was glad. I proceeded immediately and commanded the evil spirit that had entered her body to come out. She began speaking in tongues as the Spirit gave her utterance, and she was made whole. Oh! What an Awesome God we serve! He is the answer to our prayers.

> *Therefore I say unto you, What things soever ye desire,*
> *When ye pray, believe that ye receive them,*
> *And ye shall have them.*
> (Mark 11:24)

The journey through school was a very long and challenging one. Each summer that passed, I decided that I would not return. I fully believed that I had learned enough to carry me through life. Of course, that decision was always based on my own feelings; I simply disregarded how my parents felt.

Rung 2: Against My Will

My father was one of the deacons in the church and played quite a number of important roles. He was the choir director, organist, and treasurer, and performed many other church-related duties. Due to his various offices, I automatically had to toe the line. I became a devout chorister, and with a desire to excel, I got involved in every activity there was. Although I was still in high school, I was fully aware that the Holy Spirit wanted me to understand the privileges that I was entitled to. In order to partake, I had to remain sanctified and holy. Yes, I wanted to be fortified by the Spirit! Yes, I wanted to be always in His will. Yes, I wanted to be sanctified, but to be sanctified, I had to obey when I heard the voice of God.

Trust and obey, for there is no other way,
To be happy in Jesus, but to trust and obey.

As a child, I remember being in the house and hearing the voice of God, my Father speaking to me. I was often not sure of what He was saying, so I would place myself in a position to hear Him. If you think you hear God's voice, and may not be sure if it is Him, then put yourselves in a place, making sure you are not mistaken with any other voice. It is very important for us to give Him our undivided attention when He speaks.

Near the end of the last semester, a few of us were invited to spend an afternoon with one of our classmates, Dorette. I was unaware that she had a brother who was demented and had been confined to the house. I had never met him. I was only told of his condition and that he had good days when no one could tell that he had a problem. My friends and I got on the school bus and talked about our plans for the future, in addition to how excited we were to be getting out in a few months.

Finally, about mid-evening, we arrived at Dorette's house in time to sit down for dinner. Anxious to get home before dark, we did not spend much time eating. During dinner, Dorette's father and I became engaged in a conversation, during which I noticed Dorette was gone from the table. Her absence was awhile, and my anxiety rise. I thought for a moment that she had gone for a walk, so I ended the conversation with her father, and in curiosity, started wandering around the house, calling her name. I presumed that she had gone to her room. But when I looked in, she was not there. Becoming suspicious, I began asking myself these questions: *Why did I accept her invitation? Why didn't I decline?* I became frantic. Here I was in a strange house and everyone had disappeared. It seemed that I was alone.

As I made my way outside, someone pounced on me! I began yelling, kicking, and screaming as I struggled to get free. I remember shouting, "Who are you?" but my attacker did not answer, and I was overpowered by his strength. He would not let me go. In total shock, I was suddenly left wounded, angry, disoriented, exhausted, and ashamed. My uniform was disheveled and in pieces. I crouched over on the floor trying to cover myself.

Somehow I was able to gather my senses. I tied what was left of my uniform around me and hobbled out to the street. Home was two miles away, so I walked since I was unable to take public transportation. I was afraid that my parents would find out what had happened, but luck was in my favor. When I arrived home, they had already left for the market, and my siblings did not even notice my distressed state.

This incident left me cold and callous toward men. I thought that they were all animals. To young women of today, here is some friendly advice: It is not necessary for you to reveal the status of your womanhood. This is where I made my mistake. I engaged myself in conversations and foolishly disclosed that I had never had sex at the "ripe old age" of nineteen. I am sure that most girls who grew up in a Christian environment during these times were not exposed to sexual habits as they are today.

Times have changed. Sex education has now become a major part of some public school curriculum. It was my ignorance of sex that made this experience more frightening. The friends I had were obviously veterans in sexual activities, giving themselves to men before marriage. They pretended to befriend me and make it their goal for me to become like them. Nevertheless, I had a song in my heart:

I must tell Jesus all of my trials,
I cannot bear these burdens alone;
In my distress, He kindly will help me,
He ever loves and cares for His own.

It was a long and lonely road to finding myself again. I kept my encounter a secret for many years until I was spiritually delivered. At this point, my prayer life grew stronger, and I sought the Lord in a different way. I battled an oppressive spirit for a long time. This resulted in many lonely days. It was only after I had received teachings about forgiveness and learned how to forgive myself that I became free. Thanks be to God who gives us the victory! He restored my joy. I remembered this song:

But none of the ransomed ever knew
How deep were the waters crossed;
Nor how dark was the night that the Lord passed through

Ere He found His sheep that was lost.
Out in the desert He heard its cry,
Sick and helpless and ready to die
Sick and helpless and ready to die.

However, the devil did not leave me alone. He continually showed me my past so I would be held a prisoner to it. But no, sir! The Bible confirms this in (John 10:10).

The thief cometh not, but for to steal,
And to kill, and to destroy: I am come
That they might have life, and that
* they might have it more abundantly.*

So hello world! Let's not consider ourselves invulnerable. The enemy is not afraid of us. He goes about every day with unrelenting vigilance and will stop at nothing until he has his prey in custody. But Jude, the half-brother of James, says to us:

Now unto him that is able to keep you from falling,
And to present you faultless before the presence of His glory
With exceeding joy, To the only wise God our Saviour,
Be glory and majesty, dominion and power, both now and ever.
Amen.
(Jude 1:24-25)

Rung 3: The Beat of a Different Drum

*F*inally, I was marching to the beat of a drum that I had waited four years to hear. Graduation day had arrived! The auditorium was filled with parents, well-wishers, friends, and students. Mr. Francis, our principal, delivered the graduation speech. At that moment, I was not thinking about the years that I had spent at Vere Technical High School. Instead, what I saw before me was a new dawn, a new horizon, and a fresh start. Visions of ministry, work, love, marriage, happiness, parting, sorrow, motherhood, and so on flashed before me. I was ready to receive directives which were custom-made for my life. As I surrendered myself to the Infinite so that he could manifest Himself through me, I became totally His. It was then that I became fully aware of the call upon my life. After receiving our diplomas, we threw our hats and joined the class choir in singing:

Now the day is over, night is drawing nigh;
Shadows of the evening steal across the sky.
Through the long night-watches, may Thine angels spread
Their white wings above me, watching round my bed. Amen.
(Sabine Baring-Gould)

Rung 4: The Real World

With graduation now behind me, most of my classmates had moved on to college. Some migrated to foreign countries to pursue continuing education. My parents knew that I had the desire to migrate as well, but we could not afford it at that time. The working environment was a horse of a different color. Just a few days before graduating high school, I landed a bookkeeping position and went through training. Monday morning, I assumed my new duties at the West Indies Sugar Company. I soon realized that it was easier said than done. I began to reflect on positive verses in the Bible that were suited for bringing things to my memory and supplying me with knowledge. Of course, the first Scripture that popped out at me was one of my favorites:

I can do all things through Christ who strengthens me.
(Philippians 3:16)

God reminded me of a few promises that He had made to me. I focused on every song that had to do with the promises of God and began meditating on them. I knew that He was with me and would show my spirit how to handle my new job. So I began to quietly hum songs that helped me focus:

Standing on the promises of Christ my King,
Through eternal ages let His praises ring,
Glory in the highest, I will shout and sing,
Standing on the promises of God.

Also . . .

I saw the lightning flashing I heard the thunders roll,
I felt sin's breakers dashing, trying to conquer my soul.
Then I heard the voice of my Savior telling me ride on,
He promised never to leave me, never to leave me alone.

These were the times when I allowed the power of creativity and the true virtue of understanding to find their rightful places in my mind, body, and soul. They became a soothing and strengthening balm, which erased my weaknesses and gave me strength. Caribbean island residents are well familiar with the medicinal ointment "Tiger Balm." This was the healer in almost every home. When our heads hurt, we got the Tiger Balm. Toothaches, tummy pain, or anything that ailed us, we relied on Tiger Balm. It was evident that we were not tapping fully into the knowledge of Jesus Christ as our healer.

For sure, I was blessed with the knowledge and the understanding to be one of the finest bookkeepers who worked for that company. God certainly healed my mind and thoughts of anything that would not allow His child to stay focused. While working in different and difficult environments, I never lost focus of who I was. I knew that I was a child of God, called for a specific purpose. He gave me wisdom on a daily basis so that I could deal with various encounters on the job, and also at home, church, school, or at play. I was always fully aware of my God-given inner abilities and the call to do more with respect to the ministry. Constantly, I pressed toward the mark. While pressing, I encountered the bulls of Bashan (Psalm 22:12) and the beast of Ephesus (1 Corinthians 15:32). They came in all forms and from every angle.

The worst encounters that I have ever had were in the church, especially with pastors and elders. In those days, I was not aware of what sexual harassment was. It is only now, since I have grown into maturity, that my eyes are open. These individuals have a form of godliness, but have no reverent fear of God. If they were to see salvation coming down the road waving a red flag, they would not recognize it. Furthermore, they show no remorse when they enter the pulpit. They begin shouting and screaming, as if that covers up what they have done.

In one case, I was confronted by one of our senior pastors on the circuit. This person unrelentingly followed me around, wanting to carry out his inordinate act. Determined to fulfill his desires, he made several trips from the city into the country where I lived. Bear in mind, the devil is no respecter of persons. To him it does not matter who we are. His goal is to carry out his job.

Sometimes when we go against the grace and mercies of God, we cover ourselves with leaves like Adam and Eve did in the garden! But God sees us, both through us and around us – whether we are clothed or naked. The situation that transpired was this: Pastor Mischievous (this is what I will call him) wrote me a note and had it hand-delivered to my office.

Mrs. Curiosity, who was the secretary of my church and the secretary and administrator of the job where we both worked, got the note and was quite anxious to know its contents. As ignorant as I was of the devil's devices, I finagled my way around answering her. The contents were rather frightening, so I hid for quite awhile. In the meantime, Pastor Mischievous fought to accomplish his mission, even though it was an impossible one.

So as time went on, various ministers in the same circuit allowed the enemy to approach them with the same temptation, but God always gave me a way of escape. The battle is not ours; it is the Lord's. However, "*Greater is He that is in you, than He that is in the world.*" I will not say that I was never tempted, "*But will with the temptation also make a way to escape, that ye may be able to bear it*" (1 Corinthians 10:13). Let us not say, "That will never happen to me." In the earlier verses of 1 Corinthians 10, the Bible says, "*When we think we are standing, we fall. And the harms that others suffer should bring caution to us.*"

A popular old hymn says:

Yield not to temptation, for yielding is sin;
Each victory will help you some other to win;
Fight manfully onward, dark passion subdue,
Look ever to Jesus, He'll carry you through.

Many church people today are raising havoc in the assembly. You noticed that I said church people! The true Church of God does not have this sort of manifestation in its body. When God calls sinners from the deepest dye, He washes and makes them pure from all sin. He then turns us around, plants our feet on solid ground, and puts a testimony in our heart. Paul said, "*The things I used to do I do them no more.*" When a great change has occurred because we have been born again, the Holy Spirit is now in control and we do not conduct ourselves in the same way as we did in the past.

It is time that we demonstrate holiness, which should be our watchword and song. The sanctuary has become an ordinary meeting place. Many church people are only looking forward to an assembly where boy meets girl, money is collected, or pay-offs are made. It is no longer a place to hear what "saith the Lord" through His servants. As I write this book. I can hear the Supernatural saying, "*Cry aloud and spare not, show the people their sin.*"

Dr. Juanita Bynum rightly prophesied, "*When the righteous cry, God hears.*" Satan is rampant in the churches almost everywhere, causing major distractions. When the Word is being delivered, the attention God expects from us is sometimes captivated by the enemy, so we are not able to "Go ye, and make disciples of all nations," from the word, because we are distracted. We need to hear the gospel of repentance and decision, to be able to carry it everywhere to a stormy and warring world. Let us be righteous.

Rung 5: Take It Higher

God wants to see us making the effort to keep climbing, but when our efforts cease, God takes over. When I fail, I cry aloud to God! Let us cry unto the Lord. He will hear our faintest cry and He will answer.

I once was lost in sin but Jesus took me in,
And then a little light from Heaven filled my soul;
It bathed my heart in love and wrote my name above,
And just a little talk with Jesus made me whole.

This is why we do not have to make an announcement to the world when we have failed God. When we have failed Him, we must not run *from* Him, but run *to* Him. He will never turn His back on us. He stands with arms open wide to receive us.

That I may know Him,
And the power of His resurrection,
And the fellowship of His sufferings,
Being made conformable unto His death.
(Philippians 3:10)

We come to know God more by serving Him. The more we get acquainted with Him, the more we fear Him. Let us strive to become more knowledgeable of His infinite power. Let us build a communication channel exclusively for the transportation of ourselves. Let us use this way of communication to meet with God without interruptions from any foreign objects or any other creatures that may distract us. Then let us purpose to keep this channel clear so that God can flow through us. When the waterway is clear, it will be smooth sailing. Meet God at the place where He expects us to be, and then He will not have to say, *"Where art thou?"*

Channels only, blessed Master,
But with all Thy wondrous power
Flowing thro' us, Thou canst use us
Every day, and every hour.

One of the successful methods of the thriving believer is staying tuned to God in prayer! That is how you commune with Him as a friend with a friend. Most certainly, with each step you take, the Savior will definitely go before you. He sees the paths we take and orders our footsteps. He knows where we will slip along the road, long before we even get there!

Indeed, He is the Divine, the Creator of the world, the Infinite, the Supreme Majesty, the King of Kings, the Lord of Lords, and the conquering Lion of the tribe of Judah. I implore you, lift yourself to the very highest possible state of spiritual realization through the eye of the Holy Spirit and your testimony will always be:

He called me long before I heard,
Before my sinful heart was stirred,
But when I took Him at His word,
Forgiven, He lifted me.

Furthermore, let me admonish you to read the Bible daily because in the Scriptures, God does not *force* any of us to accept life. He *exhorts* us to choose the right way:

I call heaven and earth to record this day against you,
That I have set before you life and death,
Blessing and cursing: therefore choose life,
That both thou and thy seed may live.
(Deuteronomy 30:19)

Although God shows us in this Scripture our different choices – life or death – He does not leave us to really break open our brains and try to figure out which choice to make. He suggests that we choose life. If I were to act as God even for one minute, I would alter the Scripture and say, "I set before you a ladder. If you choose to climb, you will reach the top where there are treasures forevermore. As you go up, you are automatically leaving behind the cares of life. Each rung will take you higher and give you a better view of the things that you have left behind. If you choose to climb down the ladder, you are likely to grab back the things you had let go." I admonish you to keep climbing!

I'm pressing on the upward way,
New heights I'm gaining every day;
Still praying as I'm onward bound,
"Lord, plant my feet on higher ground."

I would like to refresh our minds by remembering the bountiful blessings of God. He supplies each of our needs according to His riches in glory. His desire is for us to excel in Him and look for "commencements" in our life, rather than "conclusions." It is a new dawning! Climb higher, go up another rung, and enjoy the journey! The joy of the Lord is our strength.

Chapter 2

EN ROUTE

Rung 6: Home

*T*he beginning of my Christian life was not a very exciting one to be honest. Still, I know that God divinely organized it. My siblings and I were able to get along, although all had not surrendered to God. Because we had unlike mannerism, sometimes we had heated discussions, as well as near fist-fights. However, we were always able to iron things out because we were one family.

My parents raised nine children in a three-room apartment, so we had to get along. We all had our specific chores. There was no confusion as to who would do what. I was the second of the nine children. Therefore, a little extra respect was shown to me. I was allowed to give mild orders when the chores were not carried out and give reports of who did not do his or her work in the absence of our parents.

We could not afford a lot of things, but certainly we enjoyed what we had. We were satisfied because we could not miss what we never had. The excitement, strange as it may seem, came from having just the bare necessities.

First and foremost, we would have our daily devotions, and of course I was the intercessor. It was as if I was the "elder" in the church because my family would call for me as soon as one of us would become ill. Of course, the prayer of the righteous avails much. The axis of our home spun on prayer, and I would see to it that it was carried out. At the time, my father and I were the only born-again believers; therefore, we were a little more involved than the rest of the family. We would always be going off to various services, whether at our home church or other congregations. We took part in the same activities all year round – school, work, and church – over and over again.

My father was the sole provider for the family at the time, but my mother taught herself how to survive with our small income. She would cultivate her own garden with every type of provision available. She would only purchase protein items and the bare necessities. She had no formal education or training for how to be a seamstress, but through her experiences, we learned the meaning of the proverb, "Necessity is the mother of invention." She was able to make dresses, shirts, curtains, bedspreads, and more. God brought everything together in harmony and love.

Each Christmas, we really believed that there was a real Santa Claus who was not one of our parents. We would hang our stockings the night before, and during the night we would take several sneak peeks to see if Santa had come down the chimney. He had not. However, sometime between then and the morning, Santa did come, even though we did not see him. Christmas was the happiest time in our lives. Each of us was privileged to have a whole bottle of cola champagne and hot cross buns, along with other delicacies.

During this festive season, the kitchen and the outhouse had to be in extra-spanking clean condition, with enough paper to last through the weekend and enough wood to cook with. We were not fortunate enough to have electric ranges, refrigerators, or such, but we made up for it with knowledge and ingenuity. For example, one of the best ways to preserve ice was by digging a hole in the ground, filling it with straw, laying the ice on top of it, and then covering it with more straw.

As a closely-knit family, we were able to learn so much from our mother. We were taught to be industrious around the house so that we would become better men and women in the future. Needless to say, in some marriages today, home economics are not even a consideration. Fifty percent of some of our homes are broken due to domestic violence. The young women of today should take heed of Proverbs 18:22: "*Whoso findeth a wife findeth a good thing, and obtaineth favour of the LORD.*" Finding a wife is not just for sexual satisfaction. She should be able to keep the house, and, *above all, put on the ornament of a meek and quiet spirit,* which is of great worth in the sight of God.

In the days of old, the holy women who trusted in God adorned themselves, being in subjection to their own husbands (1 Peter 3:4-5). There were times that I thought of leaving home in pursuit of a change of environment or to seek a fresh start. I thought about Mom, Dad, my siblings, and I knew that they would not be in agreement. In fact, they would probably label me as an ungrateful child. I had a comfortable life, but I was looking for something beyond what my parents were offering.

As I mentioned in the previous chapter, I saw my future at my high school graduation, and knew that it was virtually impossible to fulfill my dreams if I remained at home. Yes, I looked forward to the early morning bowl of hot cereal or the johnnycakes with bush tea. Bush tea is basically peppermint tea. My parents planted peppermint trees behind the outhouse where they grew nice and fat. The leaves were so broad that we had to use them sparingly so that we would not kill the tree in a hurry. Sometimes, when we become tired of the bush tea, I would run to the store and purchase one Lipton tea bag, and then pour two quarts of boiling water over it and let it brew for a few minutes. It made eleven mugs of tea that were satisfying to the last drop.

Each morning, we would walk three miles to school. My mother would yell at us when we got halfway up the road, reminding us to come home for lunch. I had no choice because there was no money for my siblings or myself to purchase lunch. One of the times I will never forget was when we walked home for lunch, we only had enough time to take the boiled corn and hurry back before the bell rang. Mrs. Kentish was a mean teacher so we dared not be late. She would have us stand in front of the class with our right hand holding our left ear and with our left hand holding our right toe. Oh! That was punishment, so we learned to be on time.

The times when my parents gave us lunch money, we skipped all the way to school. We were so happy! What do you think we were able to buy? Mangos! We were able to buy three apiece. We dared not allow our peers to see us making the purchase. Other entrées that could be bought were bulla cakes or a piece of sugar cane with a bottle of ice cold water.

As time went by, my life took many different turns. Only God knew what He had in the future for me, now I can honestly say that He was adding little blessings here and there. I did not see them because the transition was so gradual. It is said that when God blesses a person, He checks his or her pulse rate to see how fast it is beating before He adds some more blessing. If it is beating too fast, He reduces the blessings until we are able to handle more. So do not allow your pulse to beat too fast. Stay calm and receive the blessings of the Lord.

Rung 7: The Decision

Another year was fast coming to a close, and I remembered the promised vacation from Mr. and Mrs. Brown in New York. Immediately, without hesitation, I phoned and reminded them of their promise. After receiving the invitation letter, I had such a fear of leaving, but through prayer I confronted my fears and conquered them. My prayers were for God to make everything easy. I was afraid of changes and liked the person that I had become. I was filled with so many traditions. Leaving home was one of the hardest challenges I ever faced. Unknown to anyone, I secretly acquired the necessary documents and applied for entrance to the United States of America.

During the time of my plans to migrate, I was faced with so much opposition from the congregation where I worshipped. My position as secretary of the Young Peoples Movement was such that the congregation thought that I could not be replaced. Many reasons were given as to why I would not be able to leave. They were so convincing that I almost began to believe them. But the desire for a change never left me because I knew that God was taking me not only to a strange land but also to greater opportunities.

The parishioners I worshipped with in Jamaica had been a part of my life since I was a child. There, I was taught good Christian principles, great standards of living, high morals, when to say no, and how to protect my godly upbringing. There were many youths in the church so our pastor would always keep us abreast with the Word. He taught us not to become involved with inordinate affection before marriage, as this was against God's standards for members of the church of God. Dating was more or less nonexistent. Caught merely holding hands with the opposite sex resulted in severe discipline – the pastor would have us sit on the back pew for at least six months. Our dress had to be proper and modest, too, or we would receive the same punishment. This would not only be for us as young people – our parents would be punished equally because they were in charge of us.

At times, we would sit and discuss our futures among ourselves, trying to figure out the ways to get around the regimen of doctrinal teachings. As a Christian, I loved the Lord and would not willfully or deliberately go against the Word of God.

Rung 8: The Ring

*D*uring the time of decision-making, a gentleman from Mandeville came to my parents, asking for my hand in marriage. My parents told him that they would leave the decision up to me. However, after much praying and seeking of God's will, I was granted the visa to the United States. Great difficulties began at this point, such as the acquiring of funds for airfare. I had a place to live in New York, the necessary clothes, a new suitcase, and enough pocket money to last for a week. Plus, I already had a job waiting for me upon my arrival, but I did not have the money to purchase the airline ticket.

The visa I obtained would expire in three months. So time was definitely working against me, but a few days before the expiration date, my father succeeded in obtaining a loan which had to be paid back as soon as possible.

On Saturday evening, I began packing the few items that I had decided to take, having given away almost everything because I was en route to a land of plenty. I heard one of my sisters calling me. At first I thought that it was one of the young people coming to say a final goodbye, but to my surprise, it was Brother Big Chest. He held a lovely gift – a small box that he hid behind his back. With everyone standing there, and a silly grin on his face, he knelt down in the dust before me and asked me to marry him. Well, I began to laugh uncontrollably. Eventually, I regained my composure, but when I looked at him, he was laughing, too. He probably thought that I was happy. I expressed how sorry I was that he had come such a distance for nothing. I informed him that I could not take his ring and would never love him. I know that was very harsh, but I did not know how to handle it any better. He begged for me to accept his ring and asked me to think about his proposal while I was in the United States. I told him that perhaps I would, and that I would write him. I went back to finish my packing, because at that time, going to America was all I could think of.

Rung 9: The Flight

I boarded Pan American Airlines, and in three hours and twenty minutes, I landed at JFK International Airport in the United States of America. The Browns had alerted me that it would be a little cool. It was April, but a wintry breeze was still in the air. I was given a warm welcome at the airport. Someone handed me a coat with short stretched-out sleeves that was twice my size. At that time, I could not tell the difference between a well-worn coat and a brand new one. The Browns knew that I would not be able to tell the difference right away, but the one thing I did notice were the looks on some of the faces of the other folks waiting to collect their families and loved ones. Then I knew that something was not right with my coat.

We spent most of the evening talking about my flight, as I had never flown before. In 1970, traveling was still a wonderful thing, and something you dressed up for. I can still remember the style of the outfit I wore that day, which included gloves and a hat.

With my new family, I shared my experience with the meal that the stewardess had served, and told them after I was through eating, I asked for the check. With a chuckle, she was kind enough to explain that it was included in the fare. We had a good laugh about that, as well as how I thought there were rough roads in the sky that the planes drove over. At one point, I felt like I was still in Jamaica.

We sat on the couch and talked for a long time, and then I began wondering about my room. Mrs. Brown showed me around, and with a smile, told me I could retire when I was ready. Where is my room? I asked, then she explained that the couch I was sitting on was my bed. The bathroom would serve as a place for me to change. She threw me a blanket and assured me that I would need it.

Rung 10: A Different Culture

*A*s I reflected upon leaving Jamaica and the lifestyle that I had known, I realized that I needed to make a 180-degree turn. Prayer would be the only thing that would help me adjust to the drastic changes I would have to make in America. Someone once told me, "America the beautiful is a place where whatever one wants to become, one can become. If one wants to be a bum, they are in the right place. If one wants to excel, they are also in the right place."

One of the first things that my attention was drawn to – and I have to say, I had not noticed this anywhere in Jamaica – was the freedom that teenagers had here to smoke, regardless of where they were or who was present. Jamaican culture is somewhat different from the United States in this respect. Children are not allowed to smoke, or at least not so blatantly. I know that I will not find a Bible verse that says, "*Thou shalt not smoke.*" However, the principles of healthful living are so clearly enunciated in the Bible that no one needs to have any doubt as to what his attitude should be toward this habit. I cannot change the law or American culture, but I most certainly would have preferred if there was at least one law against youths smoking.

I remember once when our parents went away and we felt mischievous, my big brother decided that we should smoke. However, we had no cigarettes, so we made one from old newspapers. We tore a piece of paper into tiny pieces and then rolled them inside of a larger piece of paper, and then sealed it with water. He gave all of us a puff, and we were drunk for two days. Then, to top it off, our punishment was one that we would never forget.

Another difference in the two cultures is that we were not allowed to refer to our parents by their first names in Jamaica. Out of respect, we call them Mommy or Daddy. But in the United States, it is common for children to call their parents by their first names, and parents seem comfortable with this. I babysat two children who referred to their parents in this manner. I was a bit disheartened to hear them do this, but there was nothing I could do to change it.

There were so many frightening differences between Jamaica and the United States however I decided to look beyond them. I focused on my goals and the purpose for which I came, and also on the promise that I had made to my mother that I would give her a better life as soon as I was settled. I decided that I would not allow anything to deter me in any way, even though the road sometimes seemed long and winding. Sometimes my rungs seemed as though they were not able to bear the weight, but I remembered the promise in (1 Peter 5:7) "*Casting all your care upon him; for He careth for you.*"

Rung 11: The Promise

*T*here is nothing that will bring more joy than a life that is pleasing to God. The rungs that we climb should give us added pleasure, as well as fulfill our promise to Him, regardless of our beginnings. I want to encourage you to bask in the blessings that God has provided for you, His child. Each day comes with renewed promises, new decisions, new desires, and a new determination to keep climbing to greater heights. Christ has given us His mind and we will keep it as long as we remain in contact with the organizing and stabilizing qualities of the Father. He is the only one who will help us to be promise keepers.

Sometimes those that are set over us are not faithful in inquiring about our well-being, and some others are only for their own good. When I am faced with a problem, a sorrow, or a discouraging circumstance, I go to the God who dwells within me and I find solace. He certainly will not forget.

> *For the promise is unto you,*
> *And to your children, and to all that are afar off,*
> *Even as many as the LORD our God shall call.*
> (Acts 2:39)

When something is promised to us, especially if we know that it is of a great price, we do not forget it. I used to think of America as being like heaven. America was promised to me and I looked forward to that promise every day until it was fulfilled. Surprisingly, the streets were not as I had anticipated – they were not paved with gold, and there was no money growing on trees like leaves. My rude awakening came the morning after my arrival when I saw great big potholes in the streets. This was a sobering picture, reminding me that this was still not the promised place. Jesus left to go and prepare a place for us.

> *But as it is written, Eye hath not seen, nor ear heard,*
> *Neither have entered into the heart of man,*
> *The things which God hath prepared for them that love Him.*
> (1 Corinthians 2:9)

One of the most memorable prayers I ever prayed was when I submitted my application for a visitor's visa to the American Embassy in Kingston, Jamaica. Many promises were made in that prayer. I of course prayed the same prayer that many of us pray when we find ourselves in needy situations. My prayer went something like this, *"Lord, if you grant me this visa, I will serve you for the rest of my life."* Many of us have prayed similar prayers. For example, *"Lord, if you will just heal me, I will serve you for the rest of my life when I leave this hospital bed."* The problem is that as soon as our prayer requests are granted, we forget our promises.

I am no exception to this. My human nature kicked in as soon as I saw the bright lights of New York and was no longer under the watchful eye of my parents. Temptation followed me around like "white on rice" as the old folks say – "It was as if it was the order of the day." Surely, I forgot the promises that I had made, and I was certainly overtaken in more ways than I can remember. However, in fulfilling my indulgences, God never gave up on me. The Holy Spirit dealt with me until I was fully restored. God's love for us never fails. His desire for us is not to have our own will, but His will.

> *Blessed is the man that endureth temptation:*
> *For when he is tried, he shall receive the crown of life,*
> *Which the Lord hath promised to them that love Him.*
> (James 1:12)

Lord, help us to remember our promises to You, because Your promises never change. Whatever You say, You will do – You have already done it.

I remember my parents having a picture of Jesus hanging on the wall of our dining room. Whenever we entered the room, the eyes of Jesus would follow us wherever we walked. That picture served as a reminder to us the promises that we had made to our parents after receiving harsh scoldings for whatever wrongs we may have committed.

> *Whenever I am tempted, whenever clouds arise,*
> *When songs give place to sighing, when hope within me dies,*
> *I draw the closer to Him; from care He sets me free;*
> *His eye is on the sparrow, and I know He watches me*
> *His eye is on the sparrow, and I know He watches me.*

Rung 12: The Fire

*I*t was a very hot Saturday afternoon in the summer of 1971 when I was unceremoniously dismissed from the home I partially occupied – the place that had welcomed me to the United States of America months earlier. The couch that I had slept on was very comfortable, and I kept my possessions next to it in the corner on the floor.

When I returned from work that day, I did not have a clue what was coming. A misunderstanding had occurred, which at the time could not be resolved, so we parted ways. Totally unprepared, I started packing. It was nearing midnight when I finished gathering most of my belongings that I had acquired during the last few months. Then I headed for the streets. For about an hour and a half I was homeless, with no place to go. The thought of making calls from a nearby phone booth to a number of persons that I had become acquainted with crossed my mind. However, the fear of being robbed made me afraid to go inside the booth.

Finally, I developed the courage to make one call. I searched for the number of an old friend that I had met in Jamaica many years prior. At the time, she had told me, "If you ever come to America and need me, feel free to call." Remembering that, I was happy to make the call. In all of this, I was experiencing calmness, and I knew that I would be okay. I started remembering the 23rd Psalm, verses 1 and 2:

The LORD is my shepherd; I shall not want.
He maketh me to lie down in green pastures:
He leadeth me beside the still waters.

It was about one-thirty in the morning when I made the call. Edna answered with a sleepy voice. When I reminded her who I was, she seemed startled and asked me where I was. She laughed, knowing that I had come to America months ago but was just now calling her. Sensing the abandonment in my voice, she asked me what was wrong. Slowly, I told her of my dilemma, and she advised me to take a taxi to her house. To my surprise, when I arrived at Edna's, there were several other friends that she was housing as well. What a beautiful heart for someone to have! Although she was overwhelmed by the many guests, and although the landlord was very upset with her for going against their contract, she could not bear the thought of leaving me on the street without a place to stay.

I arrived at two-thirty am and Edna let me in very quietly. Her landlord was a bit nosy, so we snuck back into the very tiny, well-furnished apartment. The others were still asleep. Edna gave me a blanket and pointed to the couch in the corner. It was as if I had never left the Browns' house on Evergreen Avenue.

At daybreak when I awoke, everyone had left for work or church. Edna left a note for me with instructions about where the key was and told me to return it to the same spot if I left. I got ready for church, did as I was instructed, and left. I spent the day with a friend who made me welcome in her house for dinner. She also let me spend the night, and I went to work from there the next day.

I had left a few of my accessories at the Browns, so when I left work, I decided to go and retrieve them. I could hear the sound of a siren, and this bothered me. In the distance, I could see billows of thick black smoke racing up to the sky. Sure enough, it was the Browns' home. Everything was completely destroyed. I immediately thanked God for His direction. He preserved my life, as well as most of my personal items which I had taken with me earlier. I remembered this song:

Some through the waters, some through the flood,
Some through the fire, but all through the blood;
Some through great sorrow, but God gives a song,
In the night season and all the day long.

Immediately, I thanked God for His protection. When I was asked to give up my space, I had felt despised and rejected. My natural eyes did not see the fire coming, but God knew the future and ordered my steps accordingly. The enemy meant it for evil, but God turned it around for my good! Instead of getting mad, all praises went to God, who allowed me to overcome and go up another rung.

Rung 13: The Request

*W*hen I entered the United States, the family I lived with warned me not to inquire about obtaining permanent status. But knowing my purpose, I was determined from the get-go to immediately pursue my desire. Unknown to the Browns, I asked my employers, Mr. and Mrs. Fenniger, and it was as though they were waiting for me to ask. They were more than willing to help me. They gave me information about a reputable law firm in midtown Manhattan, and immediately helped me by submitting my documents for my status request. The Fennigers showed me love and warmth during the time I worked with them, so much so that I almost did not miss my family back in Jamaica. I was privileged to visit some landmark attractions in and around Manhattan, and for the first time, I visited a movie theater.

I entered the theater with the children that I was babysitting. I felt as though I had been swept off my feet and brought to another planet, where everyone was twice their normal size, including myself. I had never in my entire life seen such a huge screen. I was used to watching my twelve- or nineteen-inch television at home. It was black-and-white, too, but I was happy with that! This experience at the movie theater gave me something new to add to my list of things to talk about with my siblings.

Six months after I applied for my permanent visa, I had to return to Jamaica to be interviewed at the American Embassy, who granted me a permanent entrance to the United States. All praises to God for His answer to my prayer! I thanked Him for the door that He had opened and the answer to a prayer request that I had made when I graduated high school. This rung on my ladder was one of the hardest, but it was over. I basked in the fullness of God's divine promise. I could see here that my blessings were fixed and that there was nothing the devil could do about it. This achievement did not exclude me from facing obstacles, hurdles, or the devices of the enemy. As a matter of fact, this is when it all began.

I was forced to seek new employment when the Fennigers moved to Fire Island and had to give up their penthouse apartment. Everyone recommended applying through *The New York Times* because it was widely known for its large want ad section. I answered an ad for an assistant bookkeeper at a company in the Garment District, and I was invited for an interview the next day. I was selected for the position, and I kept moving up as my experience was in demand. I was young and energetic, and I held several positions in different corporations. The only expense I had was the loan my father had taken out for my airline ticket to New York.

This next job I took, I really liked, especially since it was near the best restaurants and some of the finest department stores. I enjoyed being able to walk into a shoe repair shop and wait on my shoes for just five minutes.

Rung 14: The Accident – Part 1

*O*ne day, I decided to walk home from work after getting off the train. The traffic light had just changed to green and I was proceeding to cross the street when a car came out of nowhere. I was hit, and flew across the street, landing on a fire hydrant. The people waiting to cross rushed over to see if I was okay. In the meantime, the driver sped off without inquiring about my injuries. Fortunately, one of the bystanders wrote down the license number of the vehicle. I was taken to Green Point Hospital where I was treated for minor injuries. I was referred to an accident lawyer who immediately took the case and assured me that I would be reimbursed from the Allstate Insurance Company, since this car had been registered with this agency. The recovery period took a long time, as the impact of the accident had started to take its toll. But God carried me up this rung even when I felt as though it would break any minute.

It was about one year later when I was notified by the lawyer, Mr. Phillip Werner, that the insurance company had made a proposal for a settlement, and that I should meet with him. The evening of the meeting, we met at a nearby restaurant where Mr. Werner showed me the proposal settlement and asked that I sign on the line. He assured me that when he received the check, he would contact me and set up another meeting.

Some while later, Mr. Werner notified me by telephone that the check was in his possession and that we could meet the next day at the same restaurant. I walked over to the restaurant and waited, and waited. He never showed up. I made numerous calls to his office, but he always found a way to not speak to me. Several times I went to his office at the address listed on the paperwork, but he was never there. I left several messages for him, but it was to no avail.

My expectations once again were shattered. I felt betrayed and humiliated. I have not heard from Mr. Werner since then. I tried every possible way to contact him, but I was fighting a doomed battle. He had disappeared into thin air. Now, about thirty-three years later, I have closed that chapter. God's blessings were more than any money I would have received. Certainly, there was a lesson taught to me through this ordeal. Maybe I was not trusting God enough. Maybe I had not prayed enough about this case. I had gained enough strength to keep climbing and not to be discouraged.

Take courage my soul and let us journey on,
For the night is dark, and I am far from home.
Thanks be to God, the morning light appears.
The storm is passing over, the storm is passing over.
Hallelujah!

Rung 15: The Assurance

I continued to rely on God for directions to keep a good prayer life. I knew that I would be spiritually covered. It is good to pray. It keeps us in touch with the Creator and allows us to sense His presence. This is especially true if you are alone in a place where only He can deliver you from trouble. He is an ever-present help in times of need – a friend who never lets you down. When you need Him, He is there.

My ups and downs were numerous after I migrated. I encountered many difficult times, but had made a decision to reach the place where God expected me to be. I wanted Him to show me His promises, and He did. Earlier, I confirmed that I was standing completely on His divine promises. Throughout this book, I will constantly make references to what God said that He would do. God will not allow those who trust in Him to become failures in the straightened place. God does His work. Yes! He does! This Bible is the living Word of divine activity. I will never be a failure because He lives on the inside. As long as He resides there, His Spirit is manifested through me. When I speak, it is Christ who speaks through me. When I sing, it is Christ who sings through me.

Nevertheless I live; yet not I, but Christ liveth in me.
(Galatians 2:20)

Each step takes me higher and higher.

Chapter 3

DESTINY

Rung 16: The Meeting

Trust in the LORD with all thine heart;
And lean not unto thine own understanding.
In all thy ways acknowledge Him,
And He shall direct thy paths.
(Proverbs 3:5-6)

I never know what tomorrow holds, but I know who holds my hand. I never know how treacherous the path may be, but with His hands, He is leading me. I do not have to know where I am going as long as I follow Jesus. The road to life leads to so many different places. We all have various assignments in different areas and category. When God's hand is upon our lives, not even we ourselves can control the things that we do. Even when we think that we are in control, God is the author of our lives. He wrote the book for us to use as our road map. If only we could follow that guide and see where He leads and what He wants us to accomplish.

I came to acknowledge Jesus Christ as my Savior at an early age. Many times when I listen to the old saints testify about His goodness, I wished that I had their testimony and had known God as long as they had. I saw how much they benefited from Him. I panted after the blessings that I saw around me and prayed to be kept in His will so that He would bless me too. The God who hears in secret will give an open reward. My Church home in Jamaica, the Church of the First Born was always a place where quite a number of activities occurred during the year. We would have special times when all the circuits would come together to worship in such a unique way. Believers would leave their churches near and far to come and hear these anointed preachers and be blessed.

Certainly, there was always a Word from the Lord. Spirit-filled musicians and singers would help to make a joyful noise! Indeed, the people from the adjoining communities would join in the spiritual celebration. I remembered how the lead guitarist, Cecil, would sing solos that would make everyone dance and shout as the glory of the Lord fell upon us. I also remembered my introduction to this guitarist, who shook my hand pompously and immediately asked to be served dinner during intermission. After the day's events, he gave me his contact information and suggested that we keep in touch. We would speak quite often on the telephone until he informed me of his migration to the United States. I was promised a vacation to the United States also, but it was not forthcoming. So I continued to wait. Soon after this, I applied for the visa and was granted entrance.

My thoughts were always with Cecil after I arrived in New York. Often I would find myself wishing that I could find him. One Monday evening, my phone rang. It was a childhood friend who had migrated two years earlier. She knew that I was inquiring about Cecil and had seen him over the weekend. I could not wait to make the call and was so delighted to hear his voice on the other end of the telephone. I knew from the area code that he was in Pennsylvania. We talked for a very long time and he promised to see me on the weekend. But quite a few weekends went by, and we did not see each other.

Our worship services began at eleven o'clock on Sunday morning, and the only visitor welcomed was Cecil. He was already known by our pastor and was given the opportunity to sing. Memory of years past flashed before me, and I knew that we were destined for something great. Cecil eventually moved to Brooklyn and started seeking employment. I knew then that he did not plan to return to Philadelphia at any time soon, and our friendship began to blossom. We fell in love and soon became inseparable. It was very difficult for one of us to do anything without the other. We were like two peas in a pod. We talked about the future in almost every conversation, and discussed the many things that we would like to do. We also started a singing ministry among the churches and blessed hundreds each time. At every concert we attended, he would play his guitar and I would sing.

Our popularity produced great benefits for us in the years following. Cecil's demeanor was such that you could clearly see that there was something remarkably different about him. He would not miss going to church for anything in the world and would make a fuss if I did not go. I remember the time we spent the weekend with his mother in Philadelphia a few weeks after he had moved. I was very happy to go because I knew it was going to be a quiet weekend. Boy was I wrong! While packing, he took out a suit and reminded me of church on Sunday.

Cecil was always more dedicated to church activities than I was. I would find so many excuses not to attend church, especially now that we had been labeled as always being together. We spent quality time together on the weekends, playing the guitar and rehearsing songs. We would also ride our bikes for hours in Prospect Park or drive to Philadelphia. This marked the beginning of a fun and exciting life with Cecil. He was always the first to come up with bright ideas about great entertainment and recreational activities.

Chinatown became our favorite spot. Almost every Friday night, we would go walking and shopping, and would sometimes eat on the street as we walked. One Friday night, we decided to dine at a new restaurant in Chinatown. A very nice waiter happily seated us. I ordered Coke with lemon and a Sprite for Cecil. We placed the order and waited about an hour to be served. When the meal was finally presented, it was not really to our liking. Nevertheless, we paid the bill but did not tip the waiter.

About two years later, we were in Chinatown again and decided to have dinner at the same restaurant, not remembering that it was the restaurant where we had not tipped the waiter. The service was much better this time around, in addition to the food. After dinner, when the waiter presented us with the check, we were surprised to see two separate amounts for gratuity. We inquired as to what this meant.

"The first amount is for the tip that you did not leave two years ago, and the second amount is for tonight," explained the waiter. We were speechless, but paid the bill, determined not to allow the incident to spoil our evening since it had only just begun.

We spent most of the night as usual. But when we got ready for the ride home, we found that the car engine was dead. Cecil began trying many different ways to start the car, but nothing happened. We were stuck. Sadly, we had to leave the car for the night and take the train home. All through the night, Cecil called me, moping and fussing about the car. He was so attached to his car, and it was as if his whole life had come to a halt.

On Sunday morning, we got all the necessary tools that we could carry because Cecil did not have a mechanic and we had decided that we could repair whatever was wrong ourselves. He picked me up, trusting that I could help. With much prayer, we both got underneath the car, and with a little instruction from a friend, we got the car running in no time.

We were together so much. He taught me just about everything, including sign hanging. Cecil is a sign artist by profession and many times I would be with him while he made a sign. I would proofread what he wrote to make sure there were no mistakes. When he was ready to install it, I was there with him. In all of this, we would always remember and often comment as to how we had met. I loved him deeply, but I was not able to express these feelings. I guess that it was because of my upbringing and cultural background. It was not like today when it is often okay for the female to make the proposal. I would always look forward to the next morning when Cecil would take me to the train station on his way to work. I would prepare his lunch with enough goodies to last him all day, and then I would wait for his calls as the day wore on.

This period of getting to know each other was a very close and enjoyable one. First and foremost, there was a line of demarcation that we were afraid to cross because we had such a reverential fear and respect for God and one another. It was beautiful. If Cecil decided that he was doing something that I could not be a part of, I respected his wishes and trusted his judgment. This went both ways. Although we knew how we felt about each other, we did not overreact or flaunt our freedom in any way, and did not allow our good to be spoken of as evil. We have never forgotten the training that we received from our parents and the churches we grew up in. I know that whatever we were taught was indelibly written in our hearts.

Cecil was always remembering his childhood, and even more so, his experience at the police academy. He never failed to speak of himself as the youngest police officer in the history of the Jamaica Constabulary Force to receive a strip. We knew the story so well that whenever we met the individuals to whom the story related, we were able to confirm the truth of it. Cecil also wished that the young adults of today would take part in mandatory military training before leaving home to assume any type of responsibility. Training somehow makes a difference in our society today, as the Bible states: *"Train up a child in the way he should go: and when he is old, he will not depart from it"* (Proverbs 22:6). Untrained children only become untrained adults. Most of our problems would become less if our homes would see to it that our children were trained.

Rung 17: Meeting His Mentor

Cecil and I had a lot in common so it was easy for us to communicate. He would speak quite often of his Bishop, Dr. Wilfred A. Shaw, who was the founding Bishop for the Deliverance Center Churches of God in Jamaica. The church's name was later changed to, the Full Truth Church of God. Bishop Shaw was certainly a great leader, teacher, counselor, and preacher of no mean order. Of course, we would sit for hours listening to Cecil's recollection of the many stories during his youthful guidance by his mentor Bishop Shaw.

Cecil was the official chauffeur of Dr. Shaw whenever he attended speaking engagements. Cecil did not have the privilege to be frivolous as the rest of the young people were. For instance, if Cecil was standing on the church grounds talking to any of the young ladies, they had to change positions as soon as the Bishop's car entered the premises. Bishop Shaw was a strong disciplinarian, yet at the same time, he showed so much love and interest in the youths that he pastored. In as much as he loved them, if they were not properly dressed according to the doctrine of the Church of God, and even if they resided in his house, he would not feel guilty about passing them on the side of the road as they waited for transportation to take them home.

At the death of Cecil's grandmother, I accompanied him to her funeral service in Jamaica. This was a somewhat challenging trip. Our singing together at the service was a big decision for Cecil because he knew that everyone would be anxious to know who the young woman with him from New York was. We had a long discussion prior to our trip in which he told me what my answer should be if questions were asked. He gave a beautiful tribute, and at the end, he took his guitar and announced that he would be singing a special song that his grandmother had loved. He also mentioned that he would be getting some help with the song. The song was well-rendered, and at the end of the service, people told me how beautiful we looked together and asked me my name. I felt somewhat embarrassed and questioned Cecil about his failure to introduce me as his friend from New York. Instead, I was just "some help." Nevertheless, after the funeral service and burial were over, I was formally introduced to Bishop Wilfred Shaw. This was very brief and to the point. Bishop Shaw assured me that Cecil was one of Jamaica's finest, and added that I should take good care of him. Although I had grumbled about Cecil's lack of acknowledging me, the introduction was unexpected, bearing in mind the standard of the church. I knew that he was afraid of the Bishop's reaction to the fact that a companion was accompanying him from New York.

I did not know what Bishop Shaw's reaction would be so I felt somewhat relieved after the introduction. The funeral sparked a fellowship between the bishop and me. Even in Bishop Shaw's telephone conversations with Cecil – "his son," as he called him – he would convey special greetings to me. Meeting Bishop Shaw was like a breath of fresh air. Each conversation was so spiritual, and was filled with teachings and words of wisdom. It was as though I was sitting in a classroom, taking notes, and answering and asking questions. The magnitude of his knowledge was vast and spirit-filled, and everyone who came into contact with the great prophet had a life-changing experience. It was not hard for anyone to see that Cecil's mentor was one of a kind.

Great preachers, teachers, and church administrators were birthed out of the loins of Bishop Shaw and under the leadership of the blessed Holy Spirit. He was able to install almost ninety churches in the parish of Clarendon, as well as in other parishes throughout the island of Jamaica.

Meeting Bishop Shaw for that short while brought me up several rungs on my ladder. I was able to climb past obstacles that would normally have thwarted my Christian growth and quite likely decreased my steps. He impacted my life so much that I was able to pass on what I had learned to others. Follow me as I follow Christ, he would advise us. Do not take your eyes off the prize and keep looking unto Jesus. *He is the author and finisher of our faith.* Bishop Shaw continued to encourage us by saying, "If I fail the Lord, that does not mean that you should fail also." Jesus never fails.

Jesus never fails, Jesus never fails;
Heaven and earth shall pass away,
But Jesus never fails.

There will be failures in our lives if we do not build upon the strong foundation, Christ Jesus. He is the only way. He is the truth. He is the life. The Word that He gives us is life-giving.

For God so loved the world,
That He gave His only begotten Son,
That whosoever believeth in Him
Should not perish, but have everlasting life.
(John 3:16)

The friends that we make today should be able to speak life to us. In our everyday lives, we may experience some gloom and discouragement, but these friends should help us to make the Christian life a life of love. God knows where you are and where you ought to be. Let us not try to fool Him by saying, "I cannot go on because of ugly friendships or my helplessness." The one who was helpless heard that Jesus was in town and desired to be healed, and even though he had tried so many times before, he still pressed on to become whole. Now that Jesus is here, all will be well. Unless God does something, we will become awful failures. Yet He brought us in so that His name will be glorified. He will be a friend to the friendless and a lover of our souls.

Bishop Wilfred A. Shaw was a man of dignity who was always spiritually motivated and on a spiritual high. He followed in the footsteps of his mentor, God the Father, so that he could lead the people that were entrusted to his care. Our mentor, God, has left a legacy of wealth for His people. It is all in the blueprint for us to follow in the book called the

Holy Bible. Let us follow the plan so that we can all be mentors. Let us live so that someone will pattern their life after our own as we strive to live a godly and fulfilling Christian life.

Rung 18: The Purpose

*W*hen someone dies, the year that they were born and the year that they died is written on their tombstone. The question is often asked, "What have we done between the dashes?" We all serve a purpose from the time that we enter the world. When I came to full realization of the reason for my being here, I decided that I would make a mark from the time that I was born to the day of His return.

Now there are preachers who strongly believe that we all must die. This is often heard at funeral services. I am not here to fight religion, and everyone is entitled to their own opinion. However, my statement is not based on my opinion, but rather on the Word of God. (1 Corinthians 15:51-52) says:

Behold, I show you a mystery; We shall not all sleep, but we shall all be changed, In a moment, in the twinkling of an eye, at the last trump: for the trumpet shall sound, and the dead shall be raised incorruptible, and we shall be changed.

Hallelujah! I am getting happy! The Matthew Henry Study Bible gives a beautiful interpretation of these verses: "*Bring into open light a truth dark and unknown before . . . that the saints living at our Lord's second coming will not die, but be changed.*" I mention all of that in order to make this statement: My destiny is ordained for me. It is not because God has nothing better to do than to make me, but rather, while He has me in His Hand as the Master Potter, He molds me. He has a plan for me. I can hear God saying in His mind as He works on me, "*This one I have a special assignment for. She will have many battles to fight, many hills to climb, many valleys to go through, and I know that sometimes she will think I have left her. It will be at those times when I will let her know that those sets of footprints in the sand are Mine.*" My journey to heaven gets rough sometimes. The steps became hard to climb, but this song reminds me:

Sometimes I feel I cannot . . . go one step farther on . . .
My body's growing older . . . and faltering steps begun . . .

But when I think of Jesus and what He's done for me . . .
I cry to the Rock of Ages, hide Thou me . . .

To have a testimony requires a tested life, so that others can follow my pattern and know that Jesus cannot go back on His Word. If He said that He will do it, He will! A song says, *Whatever He has done for others, He will do for you.* If we have no aim in life, then it is because we have allowed the devil to have dominion over us. Ask God what is it that He wants you to do and then do it. Be determined to get to that place that God has ordained for you. I am not preaching, but just reminding you of the reason we were created. We were made to serve the Lord. Yes, you may be in church every time the doors are opened, and sitting in every service, but He made you for a purpose. He gave you a job to do, so carry out your orders. Get busy! Stop saying that you do not know what God wants you to do. Ask Him! Remember, while He fashioned you, He had an assignment for your life.

Each of my rungs sets the pace for the next. Sometimes I can easily tell what the next one is likely to be according to the level at which I currently stand. There is a saying in Jamaica, "The higher the monkey climbs, the more he is exposed." I use that phrase in relation to my own life. Spiritually, the rung that I am standing on now has exposed me to the many things God has for me that I did not see because I was just too low to see them. I was at the bottom of the ladder and was too afraid to climb higher. Every time I took a step, I would hear what folks were saying about me, including all of the negative reasons why I should refrain from climbing.

First, people were telling me, "This is not for you." Be careful of what people will say. Many will think that you are trying to show off and wanting to move ahead of everyone else. They will ask, "What do you think you are doing? If God wants you to get that, He will bring it to you. God knows where you live and knows your number, so you don't have to rush anything." They will also say, "The humblest calf sucks the most milk –" another Jamaican cliché.

Therefore, I remained in the same position year after year, listening to what church people were saying to me. *Wait! God will tell you when to move.* Just because they were not excelling, they would do anything to stop me from moving ahead. Nevertheless, when God brought me to the full knowledge of His wealth and showed me how to rise up higher in the Scriptures, I moved.

Next, when you are at a high place in God, you cannot see the past obstacles that once held you back. Sometimes the devil brings them back to your attention. He will show you them right at that height where you are because he wants you to lose momentum and fall. Peter had his eyes on Jesus when he walked on the water. He was doing fine, but when he looked at the boisterous waves about him, he began to sink. Peter needed to stay on the level where Jesus was. He needed to stay on that high. Jesus could have prevented him from sinking, but He permitted it and made an example out of him for our learning today. I will endeavor to keep climbing against all odds, for God will guide me with His eyes.

Sometimes mid scenes of deepest gloom,
Sometimes where Eden's bowers bloom,
By waters still, o'er troubled sea,
Still 'tis His hand that leadeth me.

I know that it is rewarding to live a purposeful Christian life. Each step of the way I see the manifestation of the assignment given to me since I was in His hands. God never makes a mistake. I have never tried to take on anyone else's duty even if I think it may seem lovelier than the one I have. My prayer has always been to keep focused and try to fulfill the duties that I was created to do. My admonition to the Saints is not to lose focus. We are one in the body of Christ, and the Body has many members, although we all have separate duties to perform. The head cannot say, "I am not the eye so I will not see," nor the hand to the foot, "I am not the foot so I will not walk." There is no confusion in the human body. If the eye tears, the hand is always ready to dry the tears. This is working together as one body, performing the expected. If you are not fulfilling your purpose, you are blocking the Infinite in His desire to function in and through you, and most certainly you are living beneath your God-given privileges.

Rung 19: Courage
Be strong and of a good courage,
Fear not, nor be afraid of them:
For the LORD thy God, He it is that
doth go with thee; He will not fail thee,
Nor forsake thee.
(Deuteronomy 31:6)

*T*here are times when I find myself feeling like David in (Psalms 42:5) *"Why art thou cast down, O my soul? And why art thou disquieted in* me? Hope thou in God: for I shall yet praise Him for the help of His countenance."

It is easier to be discouraged than to be courageous. This age that we live in is unfriendly and unfair. Disappointment knocks at our doors so often. It knocked at David's door so often that he had to encourage himself. (Psalm 27:14) "*Wait on the LORD: be of good courage, and He shall strengthen thine heart: wait, I say, on the LORD.*"

> But they that wait upon the LORD
> Shall renew their strength;
> They shall mount up with wings as eagles;
> They shall run, and not be weary;
> And they shall walk, and not faint.
> (Isaiah 40:31)

Teach me, Lord, teach me how to wait!

My prayer is for God to grant me the courage I need to finish the race I have begun. The finishing line is in view and I am almost there. I will not look back. Let me encourage the athletes by saying, "*Know that the race is not given to the swift nor the battle to the strong, but be thou faithful unto death, God will give you a crown of life.*" Do not let anything shake your faith in God. You may not be the greatest sprinter, but the enthusiasm and the cheers of the Holy Spirit will stimulate you enough, and victory shall be yours.

> On the winning side, I'm on the winning side
> I'm on the winning side with Jesus;
> Though hot may be the fray,
> My soul can boldly say,
> I'm on the winning side with Jesus.

Rung 20: Strength

As I look back over my few years of living alone, I can see the many times that my physical strength was all right, while my spiritual strength suffered weakness. Of course, this is nothing to boast about. I know that I still have the Supreme Being who tells me, "*When I am weak, He is strong.*" Therefore, I fear not what the enemy can do to me, for the Lord is the strength of my life. The Holy Spirit within me is my energy to rise from weakness to potency.

Of course, I began to build back the prayer channel I once had. During this time, the devil tries to distract me whenever I begin building, by presenting different things that I could be doing at that time. Why not do it now before I forget? And so on. Yes, the telephone would ring, and many other different distractions would occur. I am strong! This is a rung that I must stand on. God will not allow me to be a weak climber when in Him lies my strength. It is wonderful to know that when we are weak, He is strong!

I am weak, but Thou art strong;
Jesus, keep me from all wrong;
I'll be satisfied as long
As I walk, let me walk close to Thee.

(Proverbs 10:29) *"The way of the LORD is strength to the upright: but destruction shall be to the workers of iniquity."* When we are strong, we have stability and firmness in the Lord. We are determined not to be moved. We shall be like a tree planted by the rivers of water. I am able to withstand the forces of the darkness of this world because God gave me the backbone that I need to go against Satan and his imps. All the powers of darkness had to flee because I come not in my power, *"For God hath not given me the spirit of fear; but of power, and of love, and of a sound mind"* (2 Timothy 1:7). Strength is power; when you are strong, you feel powerful, mighty, and all-sufficient. When the power is off, nothing works or functions. Everything shuts down.

I remember about ten years ago, I went to Jamaica to do my first recording of the album *From the Setback.* The band was there getting all ready in the studio to record when the power went off. The electricity shut down. We were crippled for hours and could not do anything until the power came on again. So it is with believers; we are powerless without Christ. We can do nothing if God shuts us down. He is our light in darkness. He is the captain of our ship, our rock in a weary land, and our shelter in the time of storm. Yes. He is that and much more. God is all-sufficient and He is my Savior.

Smith Wigglesworth was once quoted as saying, *"This is the confidence we have in Him. If we ask anything according to His will, He heareth us, and we have the petition we have desired of Him; when the Holy Spirit comes in, it is to crown Jesus King. We must dare and press on to that place where God will come forth with mighty power."* The desire to be strong is also the desire to have wisdom. Everything we need, He supplies. Ask what you will and it shall be done. Whenever you pray, let God have His way. He will fix it for you. I have learned many things in being alone with Jesus. Sometimes God needs you by yourself so that He can talk to you without interruptions. During this time, He can show you your weaknesses and how to get His fullness to remain strong. The arm of the Lord is everlasting. Many people are leaning on His arm and He has never grown tired:

What a fellowship, what a joy divine,
Leaning on the everlasting arms;
What a blessedness, what a peace is mine,
Leaning on the everlasting arms.

Every woman likes to know that she has a strong man around the house. At times it is difficult to lift or move some things when a man is not there. However, Jesus is greater than a man. One of His specialties is to lift things that are heavy, such as burdens. Call Him. He will do such a good job that you will always need Him to do it. The good thing about Him is that He will always carry your burdens for you.

Rung 21: The Proposal

I knew then that tougher rungs were ahead. There would be tough decisions to make and I could see from the distance things that were inevitable. The relationship between Cecil and I had blossomed into a beautiful flower. It was now "Honey," both ways, and not "Cecil" or "Eleanor" anymore. Sometimes we caught ourselves in public addressing each other as "Honey." I began to spend extra time in prayer so that we would make the right decisions when needed. Cecil is a professional sign artist and would always be working nonstop. He had an eight-thirty to four-thirty employment, and would work afterwards at other jobs. All this time, we would be together for hours unending.

On the weekends, church was first and foremost, whether we were in Brooklyn or Philadelphia. His mother would spend weekends with us if we were not able to go to her. Rumor had it that we were getting married – only we did not know this. We knew that we loved each other so much, hence our bonding. One Saturday Cecil visited his mother in Philadelphia. I drove to Penn Station to meet him on his return. When I saw him in the distance walking towards me, we ran like wild deer into each others' arms. Happiness overwhelmed us, we cried and laughed, and looked so silly. He said, "I will never leave you again."

Cecil would take me to the train station in the mornings and meet me in the evenings just so I would not walk or take public transportation. At this point, it was as if going to work had to be eliminated because it kept us apart too many hours. I got used to that, and loved him so much that it was beginning to be ridiculous.

Summer was fast approaching. The supervisor at work issued the vacation schedule and wanted to know when we would take our vacations. He said that he needed an answer after lunch. Mrs. Siegel had suggested earlier that I take my vacation the week after her. It was almost lunch time and I knew that Cecil would be calling soon to check up on me. A minute after twelve, my private line rang and his jolly voice came on. I mentioned the vacation schedule and told him that I needed to know his schedule so that we could go together. He assured me that he would talk with his boss and call me right back.

When he called back, we decided that the week of August twenty-second would be a good time. His exact words were, "We could take that week and *do everything*." After hanging up, I thought to myself, what is he talking about? DO EVERYTHING? What did we have to do? I was not aware of any pending concerts etc. Anxiety took over and I could not wait to meet him at the train to find out what we had to do. I believe that I was a bit naïve, but it did not dawn on me what he meant. I got in the car quickly, but did not ask him immediately. He allowed me to see how much he had missed seeing me all day. I finally got a word in, and asked, "Hon, what do we have to do for vacation? You mentioned us doing everything then?"

With a bright smile on his face, he replied, "You know, get married. What is the matter? You don't want to marry me?" That was the proposal.

On Saturday, we went to Chinatown as usual where we spent most of the evening selecting the wedding bands. Immediately, we started putting plans together for the wedding and making sure that we had all the bases covered. Everyone expected the announcement of our engagement, so it was certainly not a surprise. Everything was planned and budgeted out to the last detail. We even paid September's bills in advance so that there was nothing to worry about while we were on our honeymoon.

The Friday evening before our big day, there was so much to be done in preparation. The weekend was beautiful and we had great weather. All of our guests from out of town were already here and settled. Butterflies started fluttering about in my stomach, and tears of joy came every now and then. I was experiencing happiness. My wedding dress was hanging on the door of the closet just where I could see it. Every time I passed the doorway, I would take a quick glance at it and could not wait to be dressed. I decided that I would not be caught waiting all day at the beauty shop on the day of the wedding. So I shampooed my hair the night before, and with my rollers in, I went with Cecil early that Saturday morning to decorate the sanctuary for the wedding.

(Words and music by Mike Reid & Allen Shamlin)

For all I've been blessed with in this life
There was emptiness in me
I was imprisoned by the power of gold
But one honest touch could set me free.

Chorus:
Let the world stop turnin'
Let the sun stop burnin'
Let them tell me love's not worth going through
If it all falls apart
I will know deep in my heart
The only dream that mattered had come true
In this life, I was loved by you.

For every mountain I have climbed
Every raging river crossed
You were the treasure that I'd longed to find
Without your love I would be lost.

I know that I won't live forever, but forever I'll be loving you
In this life, I was loved by you.

To Cecil, with love, Eleanor.

Chapter 4

THE WEDDING

Rung 22: I Do

Of course I anticipated a fairy-tale wedding. I expected to live happily ever after. I knew that Cecil was the Romeo to my Juliet, and knew that he would see to it that we lived a life of bliss forever and never experience any disappointments. I could never think of anything negative because we were the perfect pair to walk down the aisle. I even dreamed the night before the wedding that Cecil fitted a silver slipper on my foot and called me Cinderella. So, naturally I awoke on my wedding day with such anticipation. I came down the stairs in my beautifully-laced bridal gown wearing old shoes for comfort.

Cecil's Lincoln Continental was parked outside the gate and had been marvelously decorated by the two of us. We did all of the decorating since he is an artist by profession and is very picky about the way things should look, especially on his wedding day. The photographer, Mr. Otis Wright, was all hyped, snapping his camera at every possible pose. As we left, the streets were lined with friends, well-wishers, and curious passersby. Dr. Roy E. Brown, the officiating pastor, asked that we be on time since he had another engagement afterward. Of course, there was a road block two blocks from the church that held us up, but it was cleared by the police just so we could go through.

Reality struck as I climb the steps of the East Flatbush Church of God. The bridal party had already done their march, and I could see Cecil standing there with such a pleasing countenance. I could read his mind through his eyes, and it said, *yes, you look great and I love you.* I flashed him back a smile that said *Thank you and I love you too.* Everyone stood to the beautiful selection "*Here Comes the Bride.*" It was pretty difficult walking down the aisle, not because my dress was getting in the way of my shoes or because I was the center of attention, but because I was overwhelmed. It was the happiest day of my life.

The Rose
(Words and music by Amanda McBroom)

Some say love, it is a river that drowns the tender reed
Some say love, it is a razor that leaves your soul to bleed
Some say love, it is a hunger, an endless aching need
I say love, it is a flower and you its only seed.

It's the heart afraid of breaking that never learns to dance
It's the dream afraid of waking that never takes the chance

It's the one who won't be taken who cannot seem to give
And the soul afraid of dying that never learns to live

When the night has been too lonely and the road has been too long
And you think that love is only for the lucky and the strong
Just remember in the winter far beneath the bitter snows
Lies the seed that with the sun's love in the spring becomes the rose.

The ceremony was great! We exchanged vows loudly, and everyone roared with laughter each time Cecil tried to break the monotony by saying something funny. When Dr. Brown pronounced us as man and wife—Mr. and Mrs. Cecil Riley—and said that Cecil may kiss the bride, this was the hardest thing for us to do because Cecil does not believe that this should be done in public, but we managed to get through it.

When we walked out of the church, we both had a smile that was a mile long. If you needed to see happiness, you were looking at it. The driver took the entire bridal party directly to Prospect Park to be photographed, and this lasted two hours. The reception hall was filled to capacity as there were guests who did not respond to the response cards, so there was standing room only. After the reception ended, some guests needed to be transported home. Almost everyone had left, and Cecil and I were still giving our last minute thanks to the guests from out of town. Someone indicated to us that our driver had left since he had to work another event.

Suddenly, someone touched my shoulder from behind. Turning to see who it was, I saw that it was Cecil. I almost could not believe what he asked me to do. I was still wearing my bridal attire with the train of the dress lying over my arm. He asked me to take a few people home because they did not have a ride and he did not want to leave them here. I guess I was too much in love to be angry – besides, nothing could devastate the happiness I felt. So I pulled the dress up, got behind the wheel, and drove them home. The nerve of some of them – when they got in the car, they began talking about how they had never been driven home by a bride. They thanked me and told me to enjoy my honeymoon.

We were the last to get home. It felt like we had attended someone else's wedding and had been asked to clean up, but it was important for us to leave the hall the way we found it. Cecil had the determination not to go until this was done, so I went along with his wishes.

This rung needed much prayer. We had now embarked on a new life, a new beginning. From here, there were many treads to climb, new experiences, difficulties, and the unexpected. Having already dedicated our lives to the Master, it was comforting to go forward. Although we did not know what the future held, we knew who held our future. Our lives were with Christ in God!

We spent our honeymoon at Disney World in Orlando, Florida. That was one of the greatest times of my life. We spent three days there, just enjoying every moment of it, loving each other, and praying that this marriage would last a lifetime through God's grace. We had read all kinds of books on marriage – ones on how to make your husband or wife happy, and whatever other books we could find. We entered into our marriage with positive attitudes. We read a survey which said that hundreds of marriages experienced difficulties because some of the main ingredients were omitted. We were not marriage counselors, but with our Christian background, we were able to apply some of what we had stored away to enhance our new life. While on our honeymoon, we made a few commitments to each other:

(1) Put God first
(2) Be honest
(3) Speak the truth
(4) Communicate as much as possible
(5) Be positive
(6) Know each other's needs
(7) Do not lay blame
(8) Compromise
(9) Forgive
(10) Keep love alive

These have been our watchwords and song. Certainly this is the advice that we have for all prospective couples. A biblical quote we use is, "*Do not allow the sun to go down on your wrought.*" Wrought simply means anger. If the sun goes down on our wrought, tomorrow will not make things better – it will only make them worse. The longer disagreements take to be addressed, the more neither person wants to deal with them. The relationship will become callous and we will walk around holding grudges and animosities in our hearts. This is where the root of bitterness starts, with unresolved issues.

The first guideline should be the Word of God. A marriage is like the birth of two children, but from different mothers' wombs. They are so different and are now joined in marriage. The Bible declares: "*Therefore shall a man leave his father and his mother, and shall cleave unto his wife: and they shall be one flesh"* (Genesis 2:24). God says that they become one flesh, but anything that is flesh is still trouble. It is proven in Genesis, at the beginning of time, that Adam and Eve were made one flesh. Eve, being in the flesh, caused disobedience, and then Adam her husband succumbed as well.

(Romans 7:5) *"For when we were in the flesh, the motions of sins, which were by the law, did work in our members to bring forth fruit unto death."* Therefore, when friction starts between couples, the oil of the Holy Spirit soothes. The couple should then come together and give themselves to fasting and prayer.

Rung 23: Elizabeth

*N*ew challenges faced us. A few months after we were married, we found out that an addition to the family was expected. This was exciting for us, and we looked forward with great anticipation. I soon developed a ritual where as soon as I was in the house after a long day at the office, I would sack out on the floor. The floor was my most comfortable space, and no matter how often Cecil would slam the doors or turn the television up high, I would stay sound asleep for at least one hour. After that, I was good to go.

The time finally came. On the Friday that it was my last day at work, the office threw me a beautiful baby shower. I went home expecting a period of anxiety and excitement before delivery. It was six o'clock Saturday morning when the discomforts began. A snowstorm did not make driving to the Beth Israel Medical Center a very easy one. Cecil broke all the traffic rules, and we were quite lucky not to be stopped by the police.

When we arrived at Beth Israel's maternity entrance forty-five minutes later, the nurse on - duty interrogated us as to whether or not we were registered there. As she questioned us, Cecil's voice rose a bit above a whisper, and became loud enough to disturb everyone at the nurses' station. He said that he would not have driven in a snowstorm, passing all of the other fine hospitals in Brooklyn, if I had not been registered there. The nurse then apologized, did the registration, and showed us to a room.

The pregnancy was a beautiful experience, and went without any problems or complications. At half past eight, Elizabeth made her way into our world. Dr. Grossman gave her a gentle slap to assure us that she was alive. This was a new phase for us, and with much preparation, counseling, and encouragement, we were able to parent her. She was christened a few months later, full of life and promises.

Here comes the tedious rung, although theoretically, it had looked good. Watching moms in soap operas on television and in the movies was a far cry from the real scene. I felt as if I were the only mother that had to learn the art of nurturing a child. Yes, childrearing is an art and a skill. Now that we were parents, we had to realize that attention and alertness would be our number one priorities. As I sat and thought about the baby, I realized that she would not become a teenager overnight. It would be a long road until then. We were the responsible parties from now on.

Many teenage pregnancies end up with unpleasant situations when reality sets in and the teen realizes that giving birth to a child is more than just having a baby. It is being responsible for another life. A few weeks after the birth of Elizabeth, she cried until two in the morning one night. We decided to put her in the baby swing, which had an automatic wind button. After putting her in the swing, we fell asleep for about three hours. When we awoke, the baby's legs were almost frozen stiff! The heat in the apartment had gone off and left it very cold. We realized the seriousness of this lack of attention and vowed that it would never happen again. This decision meant that we had to always show alertness and responsibility. With much prayer and God's help, we did it. It was like being on the job 24/7, from infancy to youth to womanhood. The good part about this new addition to the family was our Christian upbringing. The Scriptures say in Proverbs 22:6, "*Train up a child in the way he should go: and when he is old, he will not depart from it.*" From the time of Elizabeth's birth, we applied the teachings of the Word of God and this made her upbringing easier. Still, there were times when I would break down and cry when I had to spend extra time with her while Cecil did other things. He is a Christian from the heart and truly believed in the Scriptures, which say, "Do *not forsake the assembling of yourselves together.*" No matter what happened, Cecil did not miss attending church. We were not fortunate to have neighbors with whom we could leave Elizabeth, although that would have been a bad idea even if it had been possible. So wherever we were, she had to be there as well.

Our eyes watched over Elizabeth without ceasing. Yes, we knew that God's eyes were watching her, but somehow we felt that if we were not looking, something awful would happen the minute our backs were turned. As Elizabeth grew older, knowing right from wrong, there were certain disciplinary measures according to the WORD that had to be taken. Many people believes that if a child is disciplined and they continues to misbehave after several warnings, and the strap is applied, its child abuse. But disciplinary measures help children in life. They are quite likely to become more obedient, better students, decent men and women of tomorrow, with knowledge of how to give training, love, and respect. Lack of disciplining children is like giving them a loaded revolver that could be used the wrong way.

Parents today are often afraid to discipline their children. One reason is they are reflecting on what they were denied when they were youths. They allow their children to have it their way. These children become spoiled and do not know how to behave. Society will not tolerate them and therefore they become high school dropouts and find themselves up a creek without a paddle.

Although I was from a poor background, my parents gave us the best they had and taught us to be satisfied. Without training, discipline, or respect, we would become *red-eyed* – that is, wanting for ourselves everything that others have. (Philippians 4:11) reads, "*Not that I speak in respect of want: for I have learned, in whatsoever state I am, therewith to be content.*"

One of the first things that my parents taught me as a child was to "*honor your father and mother.*" This was the first commandment and it came with a promise, that it may be well with me and that my days would be long on the earth. If this advice were in effect today, I can assure you that this world would be a lot better than it is now. Parents have become so involved with extracurricular activities that they fail to pay attention to the moral and spiritual needs of their children. As godly parents, it was our job to make sure that Elizabeth grew with godly knowledge and fear. We would teach her to say grace before meals whether she was at home or at school – and to say prayers at bedtime.

The books of the Bible were a must. Each day, we tried to keep Christian consciousness and awareness around her, along with children's stories from the Bible. During the years we spent watching Elizabeth grow, I too have learned. I was able to give instructions sporadically to other young parents who also were experiencing parenting for the first time. At four years old, Elizabeth began her first experience of kindergarten. These early years were fun and exciting as she learned the basics. At the end of the day, we would always be anxious to hear about her new accomplishments. The first song she learned was:

I am a promise, I am a possibility,
I am a promise with a capital P,
I am great big bundle of potentiality.

And I am learning, learning to hear God's voice,
And I am trying to make the right choice . . .

Rung 24: The Conscript

*T*he power of the Holy Spirit is marvelous. It is limitless and can turn us around. Once we become Christians, we are not called and left at the "saving station," but must continue to go to higher levels never before experienced. I would like to share with you my experience of a presence that consumed our home a few years after our marriage. It was so infinite, sublime, awesome, loving, kind, and good. I could see that Cecil had a new attitude around the house, both for the kingdom and for himself. Even I had a mind filled with willingness to do an additional ministry. New challenges, in addition to a burst of energy that I felt to pull the devil's kingdom down, overcame me.

At first, I supposed that this new presence was because of the birth of our new baby, Elizabeth. She had brought such joy, as well as more work. Still, this eagerness for a more meaningful life engulfed us. We never discussed it or even prayed together concerning this sudden, inexplicable energy level, but we did become more and more aware that it was the Holy Spirit propelling us to that unseen level. I lay in my bed in the dark while the Holy Spirit would just minister to my spirit. When I could not speak the English language any further, He communicated with me in a language that only He understood. Bless God!

Something was taking place in our lives though we could not figure it all out. It filled our home with tranquility and serenity. One thing we knew, God was preparing us for something great. He was doing a new thing. It was as if God had given us laxatives to cleanse the impurities and unwanted residue that were concealed in us. We were basking in His fullness and getting ourselves ready for the inevitable.

This rung drafted and prepared us for the forces that would come up against us. We began to condition our minds against certain foods and drinks, being careful about the places we went and the things we participated in. Everything that was unkind, negative, and mean disappeared and was replaced by love, meekness, longsuffering, and gentleness. We could feel the fullness of the Holy Spirit dwelling within us as He continued to make rapid changes.

It may not be on the mountain's height
Or over the stormy sea;
It may not be at the battle's front

My Lord may have need of me;
But if by a still, small voice He calls
To paths I do not know,
I'll answer, dear Lord, with my hand in Yours,
I'll go where You want me to go.

Rung 25: Career Change

We had such zeal and energy to work with all the changes that God had brought to us. Elizabeth was now enrolled in school, and I seized the opportunity to change my career. I had worked many years as a full-time bookkeeper and was just becoming frustrated with the position. As I mentioned in an earlier chapter, I answered a company's ad for a full-charge bookkeeper and light office duties. No sooner had I landed the job when other duties were thrown at me. Before I knew it, I was running things. I liked it for a time, but then it became overwhelming. My constant complaint was, "Who wants to be cooped up behind a desk?" Sometimes the numbers looked as if they were jumping off of the paper. I really did not want to lose my mind trying to balance a checkbook, doing bank reconciliations, or doing the general ledger. So I decided to learn the skills of a cosmetologist. After all, I was looking for a more fun, exciting, and outgoing career that would be a more suitable outlet for this newfound energy and vigor.

The most recognized school for aspiring cosmetologists at the time was the Wilfred Academy. After much thought, I enrolled as an evening student. Certainly it was an exciting course learning how to be a beautician. I learned many interesting things about the human body. I felt at times like I was becoming a medical doctor. I had to learn about bone structure, hair follicles, nails, the makeup of the human head, ear, nose, and eyes, as well as many more details about the head. One of the things that I liked about the school was that outside clients could come and have their hair done by students at a reduced cost.

My first client requested that her hair be colored auburn. The rule was to mix the color first, and then have the supervisor check it before use. I was anxious and bypassed the required steps, going through the entire process by myself. When I was through, the color was one we did not recognize, and of course it could not be corrected at that time. There is no need to say what the outcome was.

Staying in school was a challenge, as Cecil worked full time and I had the responsibility of Elizabeth's after-school care. My first year was quite a journey. At times, I felt that I was at my breaking point, but was eager to realize the purpose for which I had enrolled. I knew that if I threw in the towel, not only would I have lost money, but all of the time and effort I had already invested in the project would have been in vain. I did much prayer and fasting in order to accomplish the new career that I was determined to have.

I was greatly encouraged when I was introduced to past students who had joined the teaching staff at Wilfred Academy. Not only were they teachers, they were also business owners who hired graduates of the academy as employees. I got the ambition to acquire my own establishment and not to be subjected to anyone's nine-to-five.

The course took two years, and at graduation, I obtained many certificates about beauty practice and cosmetology. Two years later, I applied for the state board exam. I had fears about taking the exam since I was informed that it could be challenging. Nevertheless, on the morning of the examination, I placed all my trust in the hands of God. Three days later, the Department of State, Division of Licensing Service congratulated me on acquiring my certificate as a licensed cosmetologist. Perseverance played a great role in this accomplishment, and God provided the stamina that I needed to endure.

Now that I had acquired the skills in cosmetology to make someone beautiful, I was ready to offer my services professionally. I had no fear of my ability to satisfy a client, but location was a concern. However, I decided to put a hold on owning the beauty shop I desired until I was financially ready to assume the responsibility. Now that I had a second career in the wings, for some unknown reason, the pressure of my bookkeeping position lightened somewhat. Some responsibilities were taken away, and it was as if I was leading a normal career life.

After receiving my State Board license, I would arrive at the office late with an attitude as though I had just bought the company. My head was held up high and my shoulders were back, as if to say, "Mess with me, I'll just look for the nearest exit." Wow! Not quite so; the beauty industry was really competitive. It was hard to make a start because there were so many people with the same idea. Shops were overcrowded with new students getting hands-on practice. Therefore, it was difficult to find any accommodation in a beauty salon after work at five o'clock.

The weekends were not possible, due to business of the home. I had many thoughts as to whether I had really made the right decision even though I had prayed about it. Then I received an abundant revelation as God showed Himself to me. Now, hear this, when we ask God for something, He knows when that something is not what He has in His will for us. Yet He will give us the permission to obtain it. Then, when it does not work for us, He shows us His divine will for our lives. I wanted to be a cosmetologist. I prayed and believed, because I was successful in my accomplishment! I thought that this was the additional duty God had in mind for me. I learned many lessons through this experience. Please note, whatever your goals, whether they be something academic, social, moral, or spiritual, it takes persistence against all odds to achieve them. Don't be fooled. Discouragements will face you, but the ideal way of handling them is to stay focused, put God first, and then allow Him to take control.

Rung 26: Obedience

*W*hen Abraham was ninety-nine years old, God appeared to him and said, "*Walk before me and be perfect.*" In Genesis 17:1, Abraham obeyed, and the relationship between God and himself was intimate. God called Abraham His friend (Isaiah 41:8). I became afraid as the Holy Spirit affirmed in my spirit the task that lay ahead of Cecil and me. God promised that He would not send us on a mission without the necessary equipment. In spite of everything, we had to be willing and obedient to go.

Many times, my eyes would see the thing to do and the signal was sent to my brain right away, but mentally I refused to let my hands move into action. When God told Abraham to offer Isaac as a sacrifice, I do not think for one moment that Abraham was happy about it, but he was obedient to God and probably concluded that He would provide another sacrifice in return. It was not a popular decision, but he was obeying the order.

As long as God directs us to do a particular thing, we need to do it! As Abraham was called a friend of God, we should have the same desire for God to call us His friend. We can only be His friend if we are willing and obedient. I had missed blessings time and time again because of my disobedience. I believe disobedience walks hand in hand with a stubborn will. Until I was broken of my stubborn and unwilling nature, I could not fulfill God's will.

> *When we walk with the Lord*
> *In the light of His word,*
> *What a glory He sheds on our way!*
> *When we do His good will,*
> *He abides with us still,*
> *And with all who will trust and obey.*

I have never attended training school to become a soldier or cadet, nor have I ever been enrolled in any camp to learn how to obey orders. There was a divine consciousness that comes only from God in my heart, which turned my life, my will, and my own way completely around. It was the salvation from God the Father which transformed me into this new person and created such a remarkable change. That is why I can testify:

Great change in me, great change in me
I am so happy I am so free
Jesus took me out of bondage into marvelous light,
Oh what a great change in me.

When God gave Abraham the command to sacrifice his son Isaac, Abraham was only activating an awareness of who God really was. Then God said, *"This is a man I can depend on to obey Me."* I believe that this story was written for me to learn from. If Abraham obeyed God, I ought to obey Him the same way.

The rung of obedience was a tedious one. Although at some points on my Christian journey it looks as though I cannot do what He asks, when I realize that His presence is within me, that still, small voice motivates me to follow orders. Walking in obedience eliminates any question as to whether we are in the will of God. If we are in His will, obeying Him, then whatever He promises us, we should claim. If healing is promised, please do not stop until you have received it. If the Scriptures teach purity, holiness, divine likeness, as well as overcoming under all conditions, never rest until you have overcome.

Cecil and I had to learn fully what it meant to obey God without questioning what He was asking us to do. We know it is good to ask questions, but God does not need to be interrogated when He gives us an order. If the disciples had not been obedient on the day of Pentecost, they would not have received the fulfilled promise. They willingly followed orders to wait, and continued in *"one accord in prayer and supplication."*

And suddenly there came a sound from heaven
as of a rushing mighty wind,
and it filled all the house where they were sitting.
(Acts 2:2)

The result of being obedient is empowerment for service. We should be able to go out and win the lost at any cost, doing exploits for God. The energy that Cecil and I had was ready to generate strength within all of whom we came into contact with. God showed us as He prepared us for the ministry that obedience to each other is the most important element between a husband and wife. We made a life-long commitment of walking, talking, and praying together from our wedding day until death do us part, or until Jesus returns. I knew that if we did not surrender ourselves totally to each other, the rest of our lives would be a total failure.

As the late Mrs. Coretta Scott King rightly stated, "*I did not marry a man, I married a vision.*" Certainly I loved the vision, for I saw that it was workable. How could I love the vision and not the visionary? As we awaited the next move of God with prayer and supplication, we allowed love to prevail between us. Sometimes we faced difficult days when we fell out of agreement, but we would "*never allow the sun to go down on our wrath*" (Ephesians 4: 26). Remembering all of this, we put God first in everything, following His lead in our marriage. No matter what happened, we were determined to stick together always and forever.

> *Where He may lead me I will go,*
> *For I have learned to trust Him so;*
> *And I remember 'twas for me*
> *That He was slain on Calvary.*

Rung 27: Time

God's desire was for us to be a happy and content couple, who feared Him and kept His statutes. God ordained the bringing of us together; I have absolutely no reason to doubt that. The first four years of our marriage were spent in preparation for greater things to come. Now was the time when my husband looked, to me, like a pregnant woman – he had an idea and a vision inside of him to which he had to give birth. Although I knew for a long time that he was expecting, I was somewhat apprehensive. Nevertheless, I decided to accompany him to the delivery room. The labor was a long and very painful one. No birth comes with a smile. This rung almost broke because we had been standing on it for a long time. Yes, it was badly worn, but God replaced it and we were able to make the step.

> *Each step I take my Savior goes before me*
> *And with His loving hand, He leads the way*

And with each breath I whisper "I adore thee,"
Oh what joy to walk with Him each day.

I trust in God, no matter come what may
For life eternal is in His Hand
He holds the key that opens up the way
That will lead me to the promised land.

There was a cry after awhile from the labor room of heaven, and the birth of the Freedom Hall Church of God became complete. Yes! We had an infant church and we were ready to go full speed ahead. The fruition of many promises was about ready, though the birth of our new church was still only on paper. Then God directed us to complete the call with an official ordination. This was a solemn ceremony marking the fulfillment of the call of God to the ministry.

And now, behold, I go bound in the spirit unto Jerusalem,
not knowing that things that shall befall me there.
(Acts 20:22)

Chapter 5

THE CALL

Rung 28: I Will Go

I therefore, the prisoner of the Lord,
beseech you that ye walk worthy of the vocation
wherewith ye are called,
(v.2) With all lowliness and meekness, with longsuffering,
forbearing one another in love;
(v.3) Endeavoring to keep the unity of the Spirit
in the bond of peace.
(v.4) There is one body, and one Spirit,
even as ye are called in one hope of your calling.
(Ephesians 4:1-4)

*A*s prisoners of the Lord, we were so excited about our newfound mission and most certainly not ashamed of it. It is a great calling, answering the pastoral duty to preach the gospel of Jesus and His love. We learned further how to do warfare when the enemy tries to deter or intervene. We continue to seek Him prayerfully so that we would always be able to rightly divide the Word of God.

Now, we were officially on our way into the unknown assignment, not knowing what would befall us. We only knew that our hands were in the hands *of the Man who stilled the waters;* our hands were in the hands *of the Man who calmed the sea.* Therefore what had we to fear or dread when leaning on the everlasting arms?

Our prayer requests were not for food or clothes, but for us to always continue proving ourselves as good Christians. I had prayed that God would help us to keep a meek spirit, giving us a disposition of unwillingness to provoke others and not to be easily provoked. We prayed as well for God to constantly show us the right turns to take, and to give us the correct attitude toward the different people we encountered.

Determined, I wanted to become the ideal pastor's wife. I started reading books on behavioral patterns and the type of spiritual metamorphosis to expect. My change was not peaches and cream. Some of my encounters on this step caught me completely off guard. Of course, it was a satisfying feeling for Cecil, who was now "Pastor Riley," to answer to the call that he had willfully and deliberately in the past shied away from. He knew that the task was a very great one, but did not know the extent of it. Yet he kept his determination to do the job as he stood on the promises of God.

Well, the time came, and Cecil now decided to have furniture made for the sanctuary that we had only imagined. His theory was that you had to picture some things before you actualized them. His father was a professional tradesman in carpentry and learned to build furniture. During the building and wood carving of the church's furniture, all I saw were pieces of wood and nails scattered everywhere; I had yet to see the finished product. At one point I though Papa, Cecil's father, was fresh out of ideas and the project would not be completed. I was sure that he had bitten off more than he could chew. However, in less time than I could imagine, the job was done.

The beautifully hand-carved and varnished pulpit accessories were covered from view and not shown until a place was provided for them. From time to time, as we looked for an appropriate space for a sanctuary, we held prayer services in the home of one of the new believers. In the meantime, there was hot discussion between Cecil and me about assuming this responsibility. I remember that we argued about sermons for each Sunday. I was petrified that he would not be able to preach a new one every week. You see, even to this point, I did not understand that if he was called by God then there would always be a Word from the Lord. I was excited to know that not only had Cecil been called to do this particular job, but that *he was chosen*. I knew that he was chosen to be a soldier according to (2 Timothy 2:4.) God had called us, and of course we came answering to our names, with the willing to go.

> *I'll go where you want me to go, dear Lord,*
> *O'er mountain, or plain or sea;*
> *I'll say what you want me to say, dear Lord,*
> *I'll go where you want me to go.*

We must be ready to give a quick answer to a divine call from God. We can find an example in St. Paul. It may not have appeared as a call, but Saul was on his way to persecute the Christians when God addressed him: *"Saul, Saul, why persecutest thou me?"* (Acts 9:4). God brought him to attention, and he had to listen. The design was upon him. Paul went as commissioned by God to a particular address to someone specific that he had seen in a vision. This was his first act of obedience.

Note clearly, if you believe you have been called, and are told to go, and have not moved a muscle, then you should know immediately that it is your mistake, or your disobedience. (Matthew 28:18-19) *"All power is given unto me in heaven and in earth. Go ye therefore, and teach all nations, baptizing them in the name of the Father, and of the Son, and of the Holy Ghost."* The important step here is not where you go, but how you respond before you know where you are going. If there is a lingering in your answer to the call, as to whether you should go or not go, then perhaps you are not the right person for the job. If your answer is "I'll go," then make yourself ready to execute the great commission.

The woman of Samaria met Jesus at the well. She did not wait for Him to send her with the gospel to tell others of Him. Instead, her excitement to spread the change in her life was phenomenon! Christians today should take a page from the book of the woman of Samaria. Get excited again! God saved you, picked you up, turned you around, planted your feet on solid ground, and put a song in your heart. You have a responsibility to tell others and to praise Him after all that He has done for you. Every day we should be running in the streets, shouting, "*Come see a Man.*"

There were two people possessed with devils and no one would as much as pass near where they were. When Jesus came, they knew something was about to happen. They became frightened. "*Jesus, thou Son of God? Art thou come hither to torment us before the time?*" (Matthew 8:29). When the devils were cast out of them, they ran into the city and started a testimony meeting. They had the whole city coming to meet Jesus. Notice again, Jesus did not ask the keepers of the swine to go. His miraculous act propelled them to tell others.

Matthew was at the receipt of custom when Jesus called him. Straight away, Matthew told his co-workers, "*I'll go.*" So he arose and followed Jesus. I do believe that Matthew knew that things were going to be better when he left such a good position to follow Jesus. Jesus sees what you have not seen and will never see. He takes you from better to best each time you allow yourself to be used by Him. Each time Jesus healed someone, even if He charged them not to tell anyone, it was a command that was never carried out. The recipients were always so excited that they had to spread His fame. Therefore, if you are called or delivered from any of your infirmities, you need to tell others.

We have heard the joyful sound:
Jesus saves! Jesus saves!
Spread the tidings all around:
Jesus saves! Jesus saves!
Bear the news to every land,
Climb the steeps cross the waves;
Onward 'tis our Lord's command;
Jesus saves! Jesus saves!

Waft it on the rolling tide:
Jesus saves! Jesus saves!
Tell to sinners far and wide:
Jesus saves! Jesus saves!
Sing, ye islands of the sea;
Echo back, ye ocean caves;
Earth shall keep her jubilee:
Jesus saves! Jesus saves!

Just as Peter left his fishing business to follow Jesus, I admonish all of you to follow Jesus. It will not be easy to say, "I'll go." Be aware that there will be controversy, consequences, and criticism. This call is not merely a call, but a clarion call. He is calling you today, *"If any man hear my voice, and open the door, I will come in to him, and will sup with him and He with me"* (Revelations 3:19).

Rung 29: Witnessing

And they overcame him by the blood of the Lamb,
and by the word of their testimony.
(Revelation 12:11)

Sometimes I find it difficult to witness. It is easy for me to present the gospel in songs. I rehearse them several times and know what I am singing, but for me to verbally witness comes with a struggle, especially if the right Scriptures or words do not come to mind. The Word cautions us to *study to show ourselves approved unto God* (2 Timothy 2:15). The experience of knowing Christ first gave me the start that I needed and the courage to overcome fear and take on boldness. As I focused on this, I knew that Christ's love casts out all fear. It is the desire of the enemy to bind us with fear so we do not witness to others. He creates fear in order that we find it difficult to present the gospel of Christ, especially beyond the four walls of the church.

The call that I heard many years ago brought me to Him. God spoke to me in no uncertain terms, and then I did as I was told. Ministry life is not a joke. It is not the time to buy a book entitled *The Preacher's Little Book of Jokes*. No. I honestly believe that the preacher should be down to earth of course. Yes, he should be able to bring an end to boredom if this was clouding the service before his sermon. But jokes in the pulpit have gotten so out of hand that sometimes the entire sermon is taken lightly. Sometimes the popularity of a preacher is not based on the excellence of his sermon, but by if he tells the funniest jokes. I believe that at every opportunity we should tell of Jesus and His love. Laughter is indeed necessary for the believers. It is like medicine, but sometimes the jokes are way out of hand and not becoming. When preachers become funny in the pulpit, I believe it should be something morally appealing to laugh about.

The gospel is a pleasurable deed. It should be presented in a unique and convincing way, allowing your tone and natural aura to flow and captivate the heart of any one who hears it. In conclusion, the angels rejoice as another sinner comes home.

> *I once was lost in sin but Jesus took me in,*
> *And then a little light from Heaven filled my soul;*
> *It bathed my heart in love and wrote my name above,*
> *And just a little talk with Jesus made me whole.*

We all have our different experiences, but certainly have only one Spirit. Salvation is free for whosoever desires it. So if we receive Him, let us by all means tell others. Many of us may not be privileged to travel to various parts of the world, such as Africa, China, Japan, or Central America, to name a few, but we can evangelize right where we are. God is not looking for secret servants or undercover believers. He is seeking worshippers: "*They that worship Him must worship Him in spirit and in truth*" (John 4:24). If God had a weakness, I believe it would be for worshippers. The solution to our problems will be found when we worship Him. He actually hears our faintest cry and answers even before we call. While we yet speak, He hears.

It takes much to be an impressive witness. I developed a vigilante spirit when I received the commission. I knew that wherever the enemy was, I was after him. Many times, I remembered what I had had and that he had stolen much from me. I was determined to retrieve these things. I refused to roll over, play dead, and be oblivious to his devices. The lackadaisical Christian holds back on spreading the gospel that there is a Savior who loves us and requires our hearts. God is not asking us to die for Him, but rather, to live for Him.

I remember once on the train when a young woman came on and started preaching the gospel. She proclaimed the Word, telling the commuters that Jesus was coming soon and that they needed to ask Him into their hearts. You could see how upset a few of them were while the others rejoiced and thanked God that someone had the boldness to step forward in times like these. Comfort zones and retirement homes have caused Christians to grow cold and laid back.

In the midst of the call to the ministry, major struggles came and the decisions as to where we would reside. We thought that moving to a warmer climate would be better for Cecil, as his health was threatened by the climate we were living in. While on our honeymoon in Florida, we discussed relocating. Nevertheless, it was a silent inquiry. Halfway home, we were anxious about our decision. Of course, we came to a unified agreement that we would remain in New York because of the church that we were working on opening.

My argument is not that everyone who retires becomes lackadaisical, but that too many have lost their fervor, stamina, and the will to spread the gospel. Jesus is coming soon! The Bible says that when we see these things, we should lift up our heads, for redemption draws nigh. In my daily devotions, my prayer was to be able to boldly witness to others of Him, with whom I have a personal relationship. I realized the need of spiritual utterance when God poured into me, His vessel, His anointing. I prayed that I would be able to impart the good news of Jesus and His love and that He would dismiss any undue anxieties that would prevent my witnessing. Part of our greatest assignment is to be able to lavish His love onto others, letting them know that though we were born in sin, shaped in iniquity, and are so undeserving of His love, He knows and loves us anyway.

I love to tell the story of unseen things above,
Of Jesus and His glory, of Jesus and His love.
I love to tell the story, because I know 'tis true;
It satisfies my longings as nothing else can do.

I love to tell the story, 'twill be my theme in glory,
To tell the old, old story of Jesus and His love.

I love to tell the story, for those who know it best
Seem hungering and thirsting to hear it like the rest
And when, in scenes of glory, I sing the new, new song,
'Twill be the old, old story that I have loved so long.

The joy of witnessing and the fulfillment that comes with it cannot be explained. It is like a miracle! A miracle cannot be explained or it ceases to be. The opportunity to witness is a priceless one and I tried very hard to grasp it whenever it came along. The people I moved among daily were the ones that I made a conscious effort to lead to Christ.

(2 Kings 5:1-3) states:

> Now Naaman, captain of the host of the king of Syria, was a great man with his master, and honourable, because by him the LORD had given deliverance unto Syria: he was also a mighty man in valour, but he was a leper. (v.2) And the Syrians had gone out by companies, and had brought away captive out of the land of Israel a little maid; and she waited on Naaman's wife. (v.3) And she said unto her mistress, Would God my lord were with the prophet that is in Samaria! for he would recover him of his leprosy."

The maid servant seized the opportunity because, more than all, she was a servant to God and the knowledge that she had of God gave her the courage to introduce Naaman to Him. She had all confidence that her master would be healed if he only believed. So the fearlessness to witness, wherever we are, commands God's attention and shows that He has come through for us.

I am aware that everyone has desires. That is good, or else our lives would be unfulfilled. But in the midst of our many desires, let us desire the habit to witness. I have a burden to make sure that I accomplish the requirements of Christianity. My behavior toward unbelievers is not to go about my daily routine unconcerned about them and where they will spend their long eternity. Instead, I want them to surrender to the One who gives eternal life. I feel like saying a prayer now for those who would like the boldness to tell others of the Savior and who stands at the heart's door knocking:

> Father, help us to forgive ourselves of the many failures of yesterday, and allow Your grace to make up the difference. Give us Your strength to withstand the wiles of the enemy when temptation seems strong. Help us today to maintain our promise of faith, to be able to tell others of who You are. And Father, may Your name be praised. May we see the joy before us. Roll back the eternal curtain, Lord, and show us just a glimpse into the everlasting. Keep us near You, Lord.

Witnessing, as far as some Christians are concerned, is a tedious step. Let us set aside quiet times where we ask for God's intervention and sovereignty in our everyday lives, and we shall overcome.

Rescue the perishing, care for the dying,
Snatch them in pity from sin and the grave;
Weep o'er the erring one, lift up the fallen,
Tell them of Jesus, the mighty to save.

Rescue the perishing, care for the dying,
Jesus is merciful, Jesus will save.

Rung 30: The Power

I have always been a firm believer of moving in power and in the demonstration of the Holy Spirit. Knowledge is power, and if I have power, I know I will progress. I have always striven to go up another notch in my Christian walk rather than remaining at the saving station. Let us witness at every opportunity. This is done only by obtaining the power of the Holy Spirit.

Power is a dangerous force. It is not a toy or something to play with. I remember as a child growing up on the island of Jamaica, a young man was electrocuted after climbing a pole with the effort to repair electric wires. His lifeless body fell to the ground mistakenly connecting two live wires, which had caused a power outage. Many stories have been told of tragedies caused by electrical power lines.

Power is a force that can kill you or give you life. It is beautiful when spiritually demonstrated. Wrongful use can cause spiritual power outages that will leave thousands walking in darkness or dead. Nobody likes the dark unless his or her deeds are evil, and we all need to live. So when we are called to ministry, let us ask God to give us the power to do everything. "Ye *shall receive power*" (Acts 1:8). After reading the Scriptures and seeing where all power is given to us, we held onto the authority of the Word of God and began to prophetically take positions that would make us most effective. Power restores those who have stepped out of God's will. Power heals the heart that is broken, as well as the spirit, and it strengthens the mind. It will put you in touch with the mind giver, the Holy Spirit.

Would you be free from the burden of sin?
There's power in the blood, power in the blood;
Would you o'er evil a victory win?
There's wonderful power in the blood.

There is power, power, wonder-working power
In the blood of the Lamb;

There is power, power, wonder-working power
In the precious blood of the Lamb.

Would you do service for Jesus your King?
There's power in the blood, power in the blood;
Would you live daily His praises to sing?
There's wonderful power in the blood.

In order for us to carry the powerful ministry that was about to bloom, we asked God for a double portion of His anointing. I knew the task would not be an easy one, but we had gone too far to look back. In my heart, I prayed for that new experience of the divine Holy Spirit, and when it came, it was like a lightning bolt! It filled me again, putting new words into my mouth, and giving me the eye to see when the enemy was getting ready to attack.

God gives us strength to pull down all kind of walls and strong holds from the opposing forces of hell. Many of the saints, who had promised to be with us whenever we were ready, backed down. But we held onto our confidence. As the word went out, some of our neighboring churches heard of this new venture and sought to help. We were not afraid of the devices of the enemy. All hell broke loose against us, but with our strong defense, we stood our ground. God is not a man that should lie, and whatever He told us in the beginning, we knew He would perform.

We had a deep, settled peace inside, in the midst of the opposing forces, and we found much comfort in that. There was no room for distraction. Satan came with full force against us, trying to make us lose focus, but we kept being steadfast and unmovable.

He never fails me yet, He never fails me yet
Jesus Christ never fails me yet
Anywhere I go I want the world to know
Jesus Christ never fails me yet.

In (Matthew 28:18-20,) reads, *"Jesus came and spake unto them, saying, All power is given unto me in heaven and in earth. (v.19) Go ye therefore, and teach all nations, baptizing them in the name of the Father, and of the Son, and of the Holy Ghost: (v.20) Teaching them to observe all things whatsoever I have commanded you: and, lo, I am with you alway, even unto the end of the world. Amen."* Power is authority. All of this was given to us by God. Therefore we were more than equipped to do the great commission. Go and fear not; we were called and sent by God. He gave us a message to be delivered with power and authority. This was one of His pledges, as well as that He would be right there with us.

Every time the enemy showed us failures, God showed us successes that outweighed the plan of Satan. We had the perpetual presence of Jesus Christ, without intermission. It is comforting to know that Jesus never goes on coffee breaks. He never slumbers or sleeps. He keeps His eyes on us to make sure we utilize the power He gives to us.

There are times when the Holy Spirit is longed for more than at other times. Wherever we were, our spiritual emotions search for the comfort of the Holy Spirit. I am reminded of (John 14:16)

And I will pray to the Father, and He
Shall give you another Comforter, that
He may abide with you for ever.

When the Comforter is abiding with us, He brings contentment, confidence, courage, and boldness. We should be able to command demons to come out of persons who are possessed. When we speak, "*It is not us as individuals, but it is the power in the name of Jesus.*"

There is only one way to have a progressive, prosperous ministry full of power that demonstrates the fullness of the Godhead. A powerful Christian is a prayerful Christian. We need to be intercessors for our pastors, evangelists, and all who spread the gospel to a nation needing God. Unless we are endowed with power from on high to intercede, then we will have no effect.

Prayer is not only for times when we need God to do a particular favor or when we need to do something above the ordinary. God says that we should pray without ceasing, whether we are in need or not. Praying without ceasing builds a magnanimous amount of power. We need high voltage to be able to electrocute the wattage of the enemy's devices and to remind the devourer that greater is He that is within us than he that is in the world.

Let us function only in the power and in the demonstration of the Holy Spirit. This power quickens, reveals, prevails, and is a true means of dependency. It is not the regular gadget that we switched on and off. This power is always on, perpetually available. Let us use it in the correct way. It does not matter who we are. There is no age difference or color consciousness; there are no stature or shape requirements to receive the power. This power is given to anyone. As soon as we have identified with the Savior, He turns the power on. We can use it to tread upon serpents, to destroy yokes, and to tear down Satan's kingdom. We can be conquerors and overcomers.

I was excited about having obtained this promise from the Father. When He unleashes all the volts that He has promised to us, we can move into the devil's territory and bind up his strongholds without fear. Cecil and I willed ourselves to maintain this power – we needed it! Realizing the devil is firing real live bullets, the principalities of this world will always lunge at us with a strong force.

We have an anchor that keeps the soul
Steadfast and sure while the billows roll,
Fastened to the rock which cannot move
Grounded firm and deep in the Savior's love.

Power gives authority, energy, and a more meaningful purpose, coupled with the determination that we need today which will lead to life everlasting.

We talk about the power of the blood, which is life itself. As the blood runs through the body, it sends life throughout. When there is no flow, there is no life. This power works. wonders in the blood; it saves, delivers, heals, restores, resurrects, cleanses, and so much more. The blood will never lose its power. As believers, we should demonstrate this power by showing the world that this is the same power that raised Jesus from the dead.

We should earnestly strive to activate it; it is there. All we need to do is flick the switch. Light is so powerful. The minute it enters a room or any area of darkness, it does not have to say "I'm here." You can tell. That is power! It is what we need to shine, even if we put it under a bushel.

I rode the trains in New York City for many years, and each time I waited for the train's arrival, I observed the anxiety of the commuters looking down the tracks. As the train entered the platform, there was no need for an announcement saying, "The train is coming," since it could be seen by its rays of light in the distance. The power of light penetrates the darkness for miles at a time, and the closer the train gets, the brighter the light turns out to be. The closer we get to Jesus, the more powerful we should become, and the brighter we should shine. Getting all that power from Him through the Word we should be strong enough to break down the barriers of the adversary.

Jesus wants to see an abundance of His power manifested in us. He wants to see what we are doing with it. He wants to see the flow, the action, the movement. The result is a constant ignition, if we are fully charged. Having the power does not mean that we cannot be submissive, or that if we offend someone, we cannot apologize, because that would make us appear weak and powerless. When we can face our faults and failures, and make amends, that is power. When we can forgive, that is power.

It is good that I am able to talk about the power of Christ in this manner after experiencing a refilling of the Holy Spirit, as on the day of Pentecost. This is how I can accomplish the purpose and plan God has for my life. I am yielded and my body is saturated with God, which enables me to see the revelation of His divine will each day more and more. So step on the rung of power and climb to the highest point.

Lord, as of old, at Pentecost, Thou didst Thy power display,
With cleansing, purifying flame, descend on us today.

Lord, send the old-time power, the Pentecostal power!
Thy floodgates of blessing, on us throw open wide!
Lord, send the old- time power, the Pentecostal power!
That sinners be converted and Thy name glorified!

Rung 31: The Church

*I*t was during the time of commemorating the death, burial, and resurrection of our Lord Jesus Christ that we acquired a storefront building to accommodate worship. We started working immediately to convert it into a sanctuary. As I reflect on that afternoon, I remember that a few of us drove around Brooklyn until there it was! A sign in the window read: "Store for rent." We jumped out of the car, ran across the street, and rang the bell.

After a brief conversation with the landlord, we came to an agreement on the rent which was satisfactory to Cecil. His comment was, "At least you and I can pay the rent." With the help of a few people, we were able to make the small storefront building look like a place of worship. I will not say that it was easy, but through it all, we accomplished the job that someone said could not be done.

We spent quite a few nights suggesting so many different names for the church. Some were so ridiculous that we laughed at ourselves, but finally we came to an agreement. With much planning and coming together, the official opening date of the Freedom Hall Church of God

Incorporated was set. Cecil commented that his desire was to pastor a church with a congregation whose spirit generated a free atmosphere to work.

What a joy it was on that July evening of 1981! Churches around Brooklyn and neighboring boroughs answered our request for their presence at the grand opening and dedication of the Freedom Hall Church of God. It was a great occasion, one I will remember for a long time. The opening was followed by one week of crusade meetings where many souls came to acknowledge Jesus Christ as Lord of their lives.

This rung of the ladder came with a feeling of great accomplishment. Cecil was even more satisfied than I was, because he obeyed God.

There's a call comes ringing o'er the restless waves,
Send the light, send the light.
There are souls to rescue; there are souls to save,
Send the light, send the light.

Rung 32: Great Expectation

I always looked forward to what God's next surprise would be. Oh, the excitement of beginning to experience a fulfilled life! At last, doing the Master's will and feeling good about it makes me look forward to each day with new anticipation! What now, Lord? You have never ceased to amaze me. One of the first things that He allowed me to experience while anticipating work orders was His amazing grace and mercy. "*Morning by morning new mercies I see, all I have needed Thy hands have provided, great is thy faithfulness Lord unto me.*" The God we serve is always overextending Himself to us. That is why I know that He is expecting me to do great exploits. The devil often interferes with our hopes and visions by constantly showing us discouragements, suggesting that all we did was in vain. Paul reminds us:

If in this life only we have hope in Christ,
we are of all men most miserable.
(1 Corinthians 15:19)

We are looking forward to a city whose builder and ruler is God. One day, we will inherit that mansion not made by human hands. That is why we serve God the way we do because there is great gain in store for us. I can only imagine what heaven will be like from what I have read in the Bible. The streets are paved with gold; the walls are made of jasper, the gates are made of pearl! Oh, hallelujah! I am expecting a grand entrance when I shall hear, "*Well done, thou good and faithful servant, enter in the joy of the Lord.*" I also have a pretty good idea of what hell will be like. I am not expecting to be there because hell is what God has prepared for the devil, his angels, and those who have rejected His son Jesus Christ.

This is my hope, my consolation. When we were called, we knew the ultimate reward was heaven! All of our labor, sweat, tears, sleepless nights, different church activities, travels to meetings here and there, are for one reason, and that is pointing others to the Cross and, in the end, gaining eternal life. If Jesus placed the mantle on us, and if He gave us the Great Commission, He is expecting us to commission others and so on. It is rather disappointing when someone is called to do a particular job and fails. Let us not let God down after all that He has done for us. He expects to be rewarded by seeing us meet the criteria of the blessed Word of God and live for Him completely.

> As I go winding my way to glory land, the home of the soul,
> My life is filled with sorrow where I roam, where'ere I roam
> But when I enter the gates of glory land,
> Which now is my goal, My Lord will say,
> My child you're welcome home, you're welcome home.

In order to be a good disciple, we must be obedient, staying in great expectation, continuing in one accord, and staying empowered for service. Cecil's desire always is to be an impassioned preacher, so at the deliverance of every message there is an invitation for sinners to come to the Lord, to know Him in the pardon of their sins, and to join forces with those who have that great expectation of His return.

With all the excitement of war going on around us, we are forced to lap water like men of war, looking for the enemy when he approaches, who tries to destroy us and kill our expectation. We need to be like a pregnant mother, allowing nothing to harm our unborn child. Therefore, we guard that life with our lives until the fullness of time for delivery. Also, may I remind you, do not expect to deliver if you are not pregnant. Pregnancy means a new life, and the proud parents wait with expectancy as time draws near. Although this beautiful change of the body can lead to many different results, even physical death, keep in mind that He will direct in whichever way He pleases to bring a safe delivery.

I anticipate discomforts here and there as most mothers do, but at the end of the ordeal, joy comes. During this time of our new church, I lost a lot of my friends. My appetite was not agreeing with their menus. It was easier for me not to partake than for them to change their diet.

As this was our first church, naturally the tender care and nurturing it required was no different than that of a newborn child who demands attention around the clock. As a baby grows and physical changes are seen, so it is with the church. We have seen it grow by leaps and bounds, and it has continued to grow on a daily basis. One of the promises of God was that He would add to the church daily.

A few weeks later, reality set in as the enemy stalked me left, right, and center. He had a very disgusted tone of voice and kept saying, *"What are you doing? Do you think that you can handle black people? I am going to show you that I am in control of what you just did."* Satan did not read the Scripture which says: *"He who is in you is greater than he who is in the world"* (1 John 4:4).

A glimpse at Eleanor Riley' early years!

Above:
Eleanor's
marriage to
Cecil George
Riley in 1977.

At right:
First house
at 681
Winthrop
Street,
with first
child
Elizabeth.

Above:
First child,
Elizabeth, b
February 18,
1978.

At right:
Eleanor (black skirt)
and friend.

Eleanor, 22 years old, first Passport photo.

Above: Eleanor, April 18, 1970 migration to USA.

Above: Eleanor ...ck dress), ...Jamaica, ...ears old, ...retary of ...ch youth ...artment.

At right: ...nor (left) ...d friends.

Daughters, Elizabeth and Esther.

Chapter 6
FIRST LADY

Rung 33: What is in that Name

I was elated by the term First Lady. The first time that I was ever acquainted with this name, it brought about a lifting of my eyebrow. First Lady? Why? I believed that all women of God were first. However, protocol stepped in, so I stepped back to avoid embarrassment. During a visit to another church one Sunday afternoon, the pastor's wife walked in, and as she entered the sanctuary someone announced, "Shall we all stand in respect to our pastor's wife as she makes her entrance? She is our First Lady, and we do honor her." The announcer continued, "This is the First Family of the church; while we are sleeping, they are in watch for our souls, especially our pastor." This was a satisfying answer to a prayer, and I thanked the Holy Spirit for the revelation. I began seeking the Lord for His guidance so that I would be able to conduct myself with regal pride and dignity.

I was never the one to sit in a special section or on a designer chair. If I was not recognized, it was still all right. I was just simply satisfied with my birth name Eleanor or the name Sister Riley. Many First Ladies have been known to make a stink about the way that they are addressed, especially in the presence of others. It could not be Sister so and so – it must be the title of First Lady.

It was important to be called First Lady, especially in the presence of the congregation, but I would certainly not lose a night's rest if I was not addressed that way. My name or how I am addressed is not the most important part of the service – the name of Jesus is. At His name, *every knee shall bow and every tongue confess that Jesus Christ is Lord to the glory of God.*

Sometimes we are too concerned with a title. Some evangelists will not respond if they are not called by their titles. They are known to make comments like "Who does she think she is talking to?" or "Who is he referring to? It cannot be me." We know that there are some ill-mannered people in the churches today. No matter what rules and regulations are set, they are only there to make sure the rules are broken.

May I remind you again that salvation is an individual thing? Self-discipline gives off a beautiful aura. Christians need to ask for the gift of the Holy Spirit. He will teach us all things, including protocol. When we ask Christ into our lives, our temperament does not change – it is only under new management by the Holy Spirit. I passed by a store once, and from the outside everything seemed fine, but the next week a sign was up: "Under New Management!" The windows, doors, and steps had not changed. So is it with us when we give our lives to Christ. He does not change our noses, eyes, the shapes of our mouths, or how we walk. It is His Spirit now dwelling in us that brings about a noticeable difference. The same person is now controlled by a new manager.

Therefore, if someone mistakenly omits our title as pastors' wives, rather than indulging in a temper tantrum or expressing displeasure, let's remember who we are representing and maintain a pleasant atmosphere for everyone around us. Let's behave with dignity for God, ourselves, our husbands, and the congregation.

Most of my spare time was spent on a "getting to know you" mission. It was embarrassing for me on one occasion when I went out shopping for a pair of shoes. The clerk brought the style that I selected and I tried them on. As I walked across the floor to the mirror on the other side of the wall, I saw a woman standing by me. I turned to her with a smile and asked, "Tell me, would you say this pair of shoes is fine for me?" Her reply was, "Yes, Sister Riley, they are your type of shoes." I was at a loss for words, but I hastened to reply, "Hello, how are you? Where do you go to church?" With a grin on her face, she replied, "Sister Riley, I attend Freedom Hall Church of God."

Embarrassed, I told her how ashamed I was that I had not recognized her as a member of the church. For the rest of the month, I spoke to everyone, purposely calling them by name throughout my conversations.

The hat of the First Lady is not easy to wear. There is always a focusing of my mind as soon as I close my front door and get into my car. If I had amnesia for anything else, as soon as I have to face the public or the congregation, I know then that I am representing Christ, my husband, and myself. Therefore I must stay focus.

Not every setting makes me feel comfortable. There are some affairs that I wish I did not have to attend, but representation is of utmost important. Sometimes I use the knowledge of the event as first-hand information for future conversations.

Many women mentioned the thrill that comes when being called "First Lady." But as I have stated before, I consider us all to be First Ladies. I believe that in the eyes of God we are all first, as long as we remain in Him. But protocol is a given. In the United States of America, the President's family is referred to as the First Family, and his wife as the First Lady. The children of God should not be looked upon as any less.

Conversely, it is not all in a name because the only name that matters here and now is Jesus. There is just something about that name. It makes the difference.

Jesus, Jesus, Jesus, there is something about that name
Master, Savior, Jesus like a fragrance after the rain
Jesus, Jesus, Jesus, let all heaven and earth proclaim
Kings and kingdom shall all pass away
But there's something about that name.

At one point, I was afraid to attend unusual interactions as I had a tough time keeping the conversation going and was afraid I might be embarrassed. After I did the greetings of hello, how are you, and the regular stuff, I would keep quiet or keep the conversation on the surface level. God forbid if anyone should switch to politics, in which I had no interest. Then I would be in trouble.

However, after a few meetings and seminars, and much reading, I found that things began to get better. Now I have no trouble getting involved in conversation about interesting subjects and speaking with more assurance and self-confidence. Sometimes, when I pay attention to myself speaking with authority, it brings much joy and fulfillment.

There were times when I would become fascinated by the title First Lady. Other times I hated it – it depended on the environment. I have received criticism from some people who have not matured fully past trivialities. Sometimes I would answer to their demeanor, but the Holy Spirit taught me not to react to trivial things if at all possible. At the end of the day, we are all on a level playing field, or at least have a comfortable base. I have tried very hard to strive towards maturity, with the ability to allow others to see into my head and heart. I have also learned to put my thoughts into ideas that will work not just for me, but for the body of Christ, enhancing it to its fullest capacity in an effective way.

As First Lady, I do not consider myself at any time superior because of who I am, and I willingly do my part in the daily running of the church. As a matter of fact, at the time, there was no one else to do the daily tasks, whatever they might be. And in the meantime, we had to be at every service and event. There were also programs to be typed for upcoming conventions and other events, and it was the two of us that had to do it. Cecil had purchased an old typewriter at a thrift store, and he had to punch the keys real hard to make contact with the paper. I would read and he would type. That is how we made our first convention books and programs. Another parishioner and I did the cleaning of the sanctuary. This went on for a long time, until God started adding to our congregation. A name does not matter – what matters is getting the job done.

There's a name that's dear to me,
Lifted me from misery
Took me out of sin and shame
How I love His blessed name,
It gets sweeter every day
Serving Jesus really pays.
If the Lord you've known
You should hasten to His throne
Such fulfillment you'll receive
If in Him you will believe
Life will be so sweet to you
You'll call Him sweet Jesus too.

Do not allow a title to affect your attitude before you even start. Keep your heart, mind, and thoughts centered on the lovely name of Jesus. My admonishment is that the titles we encompass now are not the important issue. Let us make sure that Jesus knows us and that our names are written in the Lamb's Book of Life. When the roll is called up yonder, every man will have to answer to his or her name rather than title, whether we like it or not.

Rung 34: Order

*N*ow that we have discussed the name factor, we can move to another aspect of the First Lady's job. The saying goes, "*Uneasy lies the head that wears the crown.*" As I have mentioned earlier, wearing the hat of the First Lady is a great responsibility. It is not just *que sera sera*, or in English, "whatever will be, will be." There is something more that is of utmost importance. It is called order.

I used to believe that order laid out in the organization should apply to everyone except me. But I learned the meaning of the phrase, "*Stay in your place, so you won't have to be put in it.*" I learned how to conduct myself. Instead of operating like I was the owner of the store, I acted like a worker working for a reward. Most of all, I had to stay focused in order to get the full understanding of what this position was all about.

Satan tried his best to deter me by presenting poor examples for me to follow. "*I looked unto the hills from whence cometh my help, my help cometh from the Lord, the Lord which made heaven and earth*" (Psalm 121:1).

From the beginning of our small church, there were some rules established. People thought that because we were young, we were ignorant of the proper running of an organization. One Sunday morning, the Holy Spirit moved among us, showering down His blessings on almost every saved individual, moving from pulpit to pew. A few visitors thought that we had taken leave of our senses, and numerous times walked to the bathrooms across the altar area. On their way back, Pastor Riley, who was now in control of the service, once more redirected them to the side aisles and beckoned for the ushers to be more alert. He also mentioned that even if his wife needed to move, she would have to use the aisle. To be an example for others is a great task, but I asked that I should become such an example for others to follow, just as I was a follower of Christ.

Another day, I walked into the church to see my husband, who was in his office counseling an engaged couple. As I proceeded to knock on the door, the secretary rushed out from her office and belted out to me, "You can't interrupt! The Bishop is counseling a couple." She was following orders and could not have cared less who I was or why I needed to talk to my husband. There were times when I did not think that I needed to adhere to every rule of the church, but I had to set a good example, not only in the eyes of those whom we were set over, but in the eyes of God.

In obeying orders, I had gained respect, and that is due every time. A life out of order only leads to a life full of failure and disappointment. God is a God of order; let us follow Him. I have always trusted God and tried never to fail Him. When I do, the pain I feel is worse than the whip from my mother's belt on my wet skin. For those of us who are from the Caribbean islands, when we were disobedient as children, our lesson was a whipping on wet skin with immediate orders to go bathe afterward. You would not want to experience this kind of punishment – cold water on hot skin – again.

As First Lady, my aim is to be enthusiastic and genuinely pleasant with everyone. In all things, I also try to keep a calm spirit and a level head, keeping in mind at all times the position that I hold and the role I am in. The desire and prayer of my heart is to be sincere and true from the heart, without any form of pretense or hypocrisy, so that the beauty of Jesus can be seen in me. This helps me to build a better relationship with both God and myself. You may wonder why anyone would need a better relationship with himself or herself. Most of the time, the self gets in the way. We can get away from anyone or anything, but we cannot get away from ourselves. Get in fellowship first with yourself.

To remain in order, often I would give myself a pep talk. No matter how strong I might feel one day, the next day I faced new challenges. Fortunately, I could go to the written Word, and hear, "*I can do all things through Christ who strengthens me"* (Philippians 3:16).

I pull myself up to my full height, put my shoulders back and head up, and begin to talk confidently to myself. I will not fail. I cannot fail. God will surely see me through. I promised myself to continue getting rid of fear on a daily basis. Every time I go to pray, I dismiss the negative areas; otherwise, I will not be able to stay in order. Every now and then fear comes and pokes me in my side, trying to make me believe that I will not be able to handle this awesome responsibility.

Trust in the LORD with all thine heart;
and lean not unto thine own understanding.
In all thy ways acknowledge him,
and he shall direct thy paths.
(Proverbs 3:5-6)

To walk in the perfect will of God not only makes us familiar with good Christian ethics, but also shows good stewardship. Jesus took me to a place of refining. I felt the refiner's fire as I went through the process. I went to the Potter's House to be made over, and all of my flaws and scars were mended.

Please be patient with me, God is not through with me yet.
When God gets through with me, I shall come forth as pure gold.

I will not allow the title of First Lady to mock me. I wear it with dignity and pride. It is not a burden to walk circumspectly; this should be my normal conduct, as well as that of every believer. Let us not walk as fools, but as the wise, redeeming the time because the days are evil. There are so many different ways that point to obeying orders and abiding in God. I know that it is sometimes difficult for Christians to follow in obedience, but it is better than sacrifice.

One of Smith Wigglesworth's life teachings was, "Let us be careful of the devices of Satan's powers, and careless when the power of God is upon us with uncertain force, so that He Himself shall be manifested, and not you."

All that matters to God is for us to allow Him. Even when we are falling, He is able to catch us before we hit the ground. Showing affection is of vital importance in the role of order in the life of the First Lady. I am familiar with believers who demand affection, yet have never shown any.

The Scripture says, "*Do unto others as we would have them do unto us.*" I find it fascinating to worship with believers who have been saved for years and who know the entire do's and don't's of the Bible, yet have difficulties complying with the Word. It is my desire to practice the precepts of the Word so that I will be able to stand against the wiles of the devil. "And that servant, which knew his Lord's will, and prepared not himself, neither did according to his will, shall be beaten with many stripes" (Luke 12:47).

As the First Lady and a pastor's wife, my stance may look very enticing from a distance – the appeal, the glamour, the recognitions, and the accolades. But all of these come with a price. My husband once asked me to do something that I was reluctant to do. He saw that I was not overjoyed about it, but proceeded to ask anyhow, and then commented, "It comes with the package."

"Package! What package?" I exclaimed. I took offense because I was already feeling the fatigue of the added responsibilities. I believed that I should be allowed to live without them. Then God reminded me in (1 Peter 5:7), "*Casting all your care upon Him; for He careth for you.*" I knew that God would not call me to the forefront and leave me to handle things for myself.

I would often feel mood swings coming on, but God's grace would temper them. Oh yes! I had my moments. Moments when I could get beside myself, and it did not matter where I was – I would always react to the swings. Again, the guiding hand of Jesus, who held the reins, reinvigorated the old me and removed whatever had triggered the mood swing.

The orders I followed were completed with a technique. I started by setting aside a time where prayer formats the day's activities. If you begin this way, just watch the results, you cannot go wrong. Pray without ceasing. Keep reminding God of His promises and what He has said in His Word that He will do for you, but do not forget to keep your part of the bargain. I am no different from anyone in the church; I have to follow the blueprint of the Bible. This I owe to myself, whether I feel like it or not. A reminder! Pay attention to yourself more. Focus on matters that are of value or edification to your place in God or in the church. In doing so, you will see when you are stepping out of line.

Show yourself friendly, ladies! Where there is friendship, there is fellowship. Where there is fellowship, there is unity. Where there is unity, there is love. Where there is love, there you will find peace. Step up to a higher definition. Hallelujah!

There comes to my heart one sweet strain
A glad and a joyous refrain
I sing it again and again
Sweet peace, the gift of God's love.

Rung 35: Mentally Ready

At this point, I had to prepare myself to speak on impromptu occasions. Mentally, I had to be ready in order not to be embarrassed publicly. When I am asked to give an address, I try to keep to the point as much as possible. By using references that fit the occasion, this allows me to not have to apologize for my lack of preparation. Let it not be said that I ever made a fool of myself. Some great advice given to me once was, "Make reading a hobby, study words and their meanings." I did not need them right away, but before I knew it, I was doing as well as could be expected.

Become a prayerful believer. Reading the Bible is a good practice at every opportunity. We do not have to be in the sanctuary or in a prayer meeting to build ourselves up. Wherever there is an opportunity—driving, shopping, washing dishes—make good use of it as much as possible. Since we are in the age of cell phones, I put my earplug in as if I am having a telephone conversation, so as not to have anyone think that I am losing it by talking to myself. When I am driving alone, this is paramount, as I am able to pray aloud and tell God my heart's hidden secrets. This is one good way to practice speaking out and even correcting yourself if you pronounce a wrong word or phrase. To be mentally ready comes with a requirement. I am required to keep my heart with all diligence; out of it are the issues of life.

With my whole heart have I sought thee:
Oh let me not wander from the commandments.
Thy word have I hid in my heart,
That I might not sin against thee.
(Psalm 119:10-11)

I knew that I was spiritually ready when Cecil was called to the ministry. However, there was a brief hesitancy until I received full assurance that I could take up the challenge. The devil wanted to make my mind his stronghold. He knew that if he could take over my thoughts, he would triumph. Darts were coming from every angle. I knew this was a test, but I also knew that as long as I kept my heart in the right position, God would take care of my mind. I was doubly careful about who and what I listened to.

As far as I am concerned, there are two types of Christians. With one type, the conversation leaves you feeling like a refreshing rain. It would be so refreshing that I would be on a high and ready for the day's activities. Their words uplifted me and removed burdens; then, I followed it up by a prayer of protection and strength. The other type of conversation would leave me drained, tired and upset from what had been deposited into me. Therefore, I knew that I had to be on high alert, guarding my conversations.

I had contemplated that once I was called First Lady, I could change people and any unpleasant behavior, and make it better. But I was not called to change people; I was called to serve, and in serving, changes would take place. Therefore, in all of this, I had to be stabilized mentally and proceed with caution. I underwent substantial changes and went through a time of adjustment; these would have taken their toll on me had it not been for praying saints. There are people who genuinely asked about my well-being. They saw to it that I was okay. They would do things to lighten the load, especially when the time came for our church's first anniversary and general assembly.

Encouraging comments came from other pastors' wives as they congratulated me for the leap of faith and boldness. This was a bright spot in my new experience, and to God be the glory. However, the true praise and sanctioning word must come from the Holy Spirit. This readiness felt like a beautiful sunny day that came to warm the soul in the midst of winter, or like a glass of lemonade on a hot day when all one can think about is that drink. When all is said and done, it felt like autumn when the leaves gather in different shades of gold, singing praises to the King of Kings and Lord of Lords.

In my private prayer, I asked God to keep me consciously ready, and to be always in tune with the needs and longing of my heart as it pants for him, and for me to be kept from causing offense to others.

This is a tough prayer because it is hard not to offend. Sometimes when I assume that all should be pleased with me for my dedication, willingness, and hard work, people say that I just want to do it all by myself. But in the middle of sarcasm, I'm kept from the indifference of the ones who express only hypocrisy. I have learned to pray in a different way since I began this new walk. No longer do I pray for men to be removed, but for God to move those who fight against me. Man without

God is nothing, but God without man remains God. That should be the design of our prayer.

The success of any child of God is based on the strength of his or her prayer life. This kindles a fervent thirst for all spiritual blessings. God warns me to have His mind, so in spite of whatever comes, I will love. Love "*seeketh not her own.*" I can do absolutely nothing without Christ, even to be an effective First Lady. It is through the Holy Spirit that I am able to do all things. I believe I can.

I consider myself a woman of fortune even without being married to the world's richest man or becoming the First Lady of the United States of America or any other highly-rated position. I consider myself to be a friend to the friendless, a comfort to those who need comforting, and a giver of bread to the hungry. By being these things, I stand a good chance of winning them for Christ. I did not ask for my portion of goods or to leave home, nor did I waste my substance on riotous living, because I had nothing. I was saved at a tender age of ten years. My struggles were great, but God provided for me. All that I knew was to work in the church at whatever my hands seemed fit to do.

In conducting myself as much as possible without strain or stress, I bear in mind that the inspiration is more than the operation. I must be inspired in speaking, in worship, in work, and in song. Without these, I am of no effect and no power. My thought was that if I could just be effective, our congregation would soon grow in great numbers.

If I find myself so involved in the mission of adding to the church daily, I shall offer no apology. I believe that I will never be tolerated by a congregation if I am not guided by wisdom, which is the gift of the Spirit. To maintain a good relationship with God is always healthy in every way. I must not at any time cause God to query, "*Eleanor, where art thou?*" I am living in a world now that may not be the Garden of Eden, but I have greater access to the triune God which allows me to stay constantly in His presence.

In thy presence is fullness of joy;
at thy right hand there are pleasures
forevermore.
(Psalm 16:11)

My desire is for Him who loved us so, that when He left the splendors of heaven and become incarnate, seeking and saving that which was lost, I was thought of. I am overwhelmed every time I think of what Jesus went through for me. Heaven is full of majesty, adoration, tranquility and divine love, and no matter how boisterous it is here on earth, heaven is not shaken. We cannot interrupt the setting or the serenity there. God is still fixing things to receive us. When our mansion is finished, we will be inheriting the most beautiful reward – one not made by hands. Hallelujah, praise the Lord!

My foundation determines everything. Even in our churches today, there are some who build their foundations not upon gold, silver, or precious stones, but upon wood, hay, and stubble. Let us try our best to focus more on Christ, who is the Ruler and Head of the Church. Our purpose is to build on Him, the sure foundation.

I pray that I will not be exalted, but remain humble, leaving much room for penitence and crying before God, with fasting and prayer. I believe that if I want to be an exemplary First Lady, I must be consistent in everything that I do, as well as remain loyal and obedient to Christ. I will be effective because I have fully trusted Him as my all in all. There is no other support that I lean on. The arms of flesh will fail me, and I dare not trust my own. It is only when I lean upon the everlasting arm of Jesus that I trust. *"God has not given us the spirit of fear, but of power, of love and of a sound mind"* (2 Timothy 1:7). The worst treachery is to permit any human power to come between my God and me.

Do we really know Christ? This is the supreme question for our churches and ourselves. Is it enough that we know Christ Himself by the mere report of others? Or should we know Him for ourselves? What others have told us of Him is not enough. We must spread this news of salvation throughout the world because we have heard it from His own lips. Let us, when we testify of Him and His goodness, speak as witnesses of the King of Kings.

My whole nature, my whole ministry, must be penetrated and transfigured with His glory. As the First Lady, I pray that this direct and supernatural revelation of Christ may be made to all of us.

Keep climbing.

Rung 36: The Christian Life

My buddies tell me, that I have waited
They say I'm missing a whole world of fun
But I am happy and I sing with pride
I like the Christian life.

I won't lose a friend by heeding God's call
For who is a friend who would want you to fall
Others find pleasure in things I despised
I like the Christian Life.

Someone once wrote, "If heaven was never promised to us, it still would have been worth having the Lord on our side. I am redeemed, bought with a price; Jesus has changed my whole life; if anybody asks you just who I am, tell them I am redeemed." Salvation was given to us by God Himself to redeem mankind from sin. *Hallelujah, what a Savior, Hallelujah, what a Savior.*

Why do I like the Christian life? To answer this question, let us carefully examine what the Word of God says, since it carries an endless wealth of information. The Scripture tells us we will find "eternal life." Eternal life can only be inherited by those who not only live the Christian life, but who have also confessed Christ in the pardoning of our sin and have decided to walk in the newness of life. There is only one way to live a Christian life. There is no middle ground. We must become devout believers by reading His Word and participating in daily prayers and intercessory communication with the Lord. If we have made up our mind to serve the Lord with all of our hearts, we surely will enjoy living the Christian life.

There are believers who confess how hard it is to live the Christian life. They struggle with the "do's and don't's" at regular intervals. When you accept Jesus Christ into your life, please be assured that He is able to keep you. *"If Christ be in you, the body is dead because of sin, but the spirit is life because of righteousness."*

To be born again is a personal encounter with the Holy Spirit, who does the drawing. The Word of God says, *"And I, if I be lifted up . . . I will draw all men unto me."* One has to have the experience to be able to testify to it in sharing the good news of Jesus and His love. I have not had any experience so personal, so life changing, so challenging and serene, as when I surrender to the Lord. The Christian life has no regrets, no failures, or disappointments. I cherish the relationship that I have with God, and someday I will see Him face to face to thank Him for His love. I came to despise many things that I had loved a lot. Though others find much pleasure in them, I would rather have the Christian life.

At age ten, I was mature enough to differentiate right from wrong. My conscience would keep me aware of anything that was not right. I was kept in subjection, which has lasted until today. The life I live now is a constant pageant of triumph in God. I am always striving to be an overcomer, rather than a coward. Being on the battlefield, I have learned to fight, knowing that I am not up against flesh and blood, but against principalities, the powers of darkness, and the wiles of the enemy. I was taught this by the Holy Spirit ever since I accepted Christ as my personal Lord and Savior.

The desire to keep a conquering spirit like Paul is strong in me. I use his words of encouragement so that at the end of life's journey, I can say for a fact that "*I have fought a good fight, I have finished my course, I have kept the faith: henceforth there is laid up for me a crown of righteousness, which the Lord, the righteous judge, shall give me at that day: and not to me only, but unto all them also that love His appearing*" (2 Timothy 4:7-8). What an award ceremony that will be! It will be the biggest one there ever was. Crowns – not high school diplomas, not doctorate degrees, not Oscars or Emmys – will be handed out. Hallelujah!

Sometimes when I watch the award shows, I feel joy for those who win. But I know that the day is coming when my reward will not be achieved in a competitive way, but in a way that will be well-pleasing in His sight. My desire when I arrive at the end of my life's journey is to stand before my Redeemer and thank Him for His salvation plan. If it was not for that plan, I would be nothing. My life would be worthless. Thank God He made the difference.

I have a desire for my spiritual life to bud, bloom, and blossom into beauty, which begins with our creator, JESUS CHRIST, the Righteous One, who gave His life for us. Many have entered the race and failed. They have laid blame everywhere except on themselves. "The devil made me do it" is no longer an acceptable excuse. Those were the days when sympathy could sneak in, and the focus was no longer on the situation, but on the deed. Today, we are held responsible for whatever is done in the body. We ought to make men tremble when we reason with them about salvation, righteousness, temperance, and the judgment to come. Somebody once exclaimed, "The Christian life is more than to be liked," it should be, "I love the Christian life!"

My passion as the First Lady of the Freedom Hall Church of God in Brooklyn, New York, is to be able to communicate with other First Ladies from various churches, to have one-on-one dialogue with them, and to come together in unity with the determination to set an example for the younger women, showing them how to be decent, upright, and behave as women of God. They do not have to go with the flow; anyone can go with the flow. As I mentioned in an earlier chapter, it takes life, strength, and courage to go *against* the flow.

We need a society of decent women – women with dignity, self-esteem, and a powerful will – to be positive leaders in their communities, handing down the baton from generation to generation with respect and loyalty. Young women should be trained in this way from childhood, guided well in God's will. In due season, they shall become a helpmate to someone who is called by God to a ministry as a shepherd, answering the call, as Cecil did, to be a light carrier shining on to that perfect day.

Folks once thought that because I am the pastor's wife, I have moved to live on Easy Street with Contentment Circle outlining my cottage. If only they could see the responsibility that comes with this title, they would not desire to change their lot for mine. If a made-up mind does not accompany faithfulness, it will ignore the true meaning of living the Christian life.

It is my desire to walk hand-in-hand with Jesus; when walking with Him, I cannot stray. I refuse to be like the unruly child, pulling every which way but loose, stubborn and in my own will. I remember when I would sing: "*Have thine own way Lord, have thine own way, thou art the potter, I am the clay, mold me and make me after thy will, while in thy presence yielded and still.*" I would sing this song because I knew the tune and words well, but I took note of the message that it sent so forcefully to my spirit, feeling my heart beating with joy in response to allowing him to have His own way, my hand was kept in His.

As the forces continued coming against me, if I was not allowing the Holy Spirit to take control to mold me and make me after His will, this First Lady would harbor unkind and unjust acts done to me and quite likely would take action.

These forces were not only in the church where my husband pastored, but outside of it as well. The relationship that I had with many of my so-called friends changed as I came face to face with them in what real friendship should be. I worshipped with some of them, and even connected myself more with the ones that I thought were real. We ate at the same table, and sometimes drank from the same cup. When we think we know who people are, wait until one is promoted or blessed a little more than they think we should be, then we will ask, "Will the real Mr. or Ms. So-and-So, please stand up?"

I came to the place where I almost regretted being the First Lady. I started looking back over my life and began to wish for the days when I was just ordinary me, just Eleanor. I would think that I was more at peace with myself and with God then. I was ready to give my concession speech, but just in the nick of time, Jesus intervened on my behalf and reminded me of why He had promoted me to this level.

By this time, the changes in some of the ladies were startling, and this caused me to raise an eyebrow. There was a time that I could request a favor and it was done without murmur, but it came to the point where they would not lift a finger anymore because they were now allowing the enemy to fill their heart with resentment and jealousy. Instead of helping to make the load lighter, they would say, with sarcasm, "We are all First Ladies."

Despite all of the things that I have gone through, I am still here. Many nights, I envisioned getting into a rage and blowing my good record, but He gave me presence of mind. Not only did He bring presence of mind, He once again reminded me of His promises: "*I will never leave you nor forsake you; I will be with you alway.*"

Thank God for the morning light, which not only brings the daybreak so that I can see the sunlight, but which also brings light for my spirit to comprehend what He wants me to see in Him, lighting the unknown path that I take.

Chapter 7

TO SHARE OR NOT

TO SHARE

Rung 37: Sharing

*B*ecause of the ministry, I learned new behavioral patterns and learned how to deal with fresh changes. I had to learn to share many of the things that I loved, although I was comfortable having these things all to myself. I am not just speaking of spiritual sharing, but of sharing as a whole. Formerly, the focus would have been on "I," but now, as a part of the family of God, we must change that agenda to include others, whether they are believers or not. One way in which I changed my "I" to "we" was through cooking.

I make different dishes for various occasions, and when doing so, I always have someone in mind to share it with, either a member of our congregation, the tenants in our home, or a co-worker. One of my favorite pastries is cornbread. Everyone gets a mouth-watering craving for a slice of it, particularly on rainy mornings. My favorite dish is a delicious turkey loaf, along with some real Jamaican carrot juice. It is my signature dish for Thanksgiving or Christmas. It is always a beautiful thing to give of yourself and make someone feel like they belong at the same time.

I systematically learned the teachings of the Bible. I also learned how to fellowship and how to share some of the things that God has blessed me with, "For it is by giving that I am blessed." It isn't always easy, but He provides often, and in mysterious ways, in order to prove to His people that He is the great provider. He will make a way out of nowhere.

Sometimes I would feel a little apprehensive about an individual that I had previously helped. I have seen people come to us, wanting to be a part of our organization, and in a few weeks, as soon as they have been helped, they have gone to another. Although I have the heart to help and a constant desire to share, many times we were taken advantage of. But holding on to this world's goods with an iron fist is not fulfilling the Word of God; instead, our hearts must be filled with compassion always, and we must be without selfishness. For a moment, I might refuse a request, but soon after, I will be reaching down with a helping hand.

Finally, be ye all of one mind,
having compassion one of another,
love as congregation, be pitiful, be courteous.
(1 Peter 3:8)

Cecil and I bought our house on Winthrop Street soon after we were married. It was my castle, my domain. My husband honored me as his queen, and I held him in high esteem as the king of our home. He is a man who really knows how to take care of his family, and he gives us a sense of belonging at all times. The décor of our castle was unique and always drew the attention of anyone who visited. It was not on a hundred acres of land, nor did it have a swimming pool or tennis court. It was situated on a busy street, surrounded by hospitals. However, the quiet within was awesome, lovely, and breathtaking. It was a place where love was felt at all times. The homey atmosphere made it difficult for any visitor to leave.

During those years, I learned to be careful with the blessings of the Lord. As someone said, "When the Lord blesses, He checks our pulse. If it races, then He cuts back until we are able to handle more blessings." I truly believe that when one is blessed, it is not for him or her to be selfish, but to share with others who may be less fortunate. I am able to sleep, eat, and digest meals without pain or discomfort because of the inner peace that I have, knowing that I am in the Master's will.

"I have shewed you all things, how that so labouring ye ought to support the weak, and to remember the words of the Lord Jesus, how he said, "It is more blessed to give than to receive."
(Acts 20:35)

Cecil always shows his love in unusual and unique ways. One day, he took a new direction driving to work, and his eyes fell on a round bed in the show window of a furniture store on Broadway in Brooklyn. Immediately, he fell in love with the bed and decided to purchase it. After dinner that evening, he told me that he had a surprise and invited me to take a drive with him. When I saw the bed, I was filled with delight, as I had never seen a round one before.

I cherished our new purchase and treated it with care. Because we were in the ministry, on many occasions we had to give up the luxurious round bed for the living room floor. Because of the layout of our house, one couldn't tell that we did not have another bedroom.

Elizabeth had her room, but it was not an option to have anyone else sleeping there. Though we had two apartments upstairs, they were rented out. We continued to share as the need arose and until everyone was comfortable and happy.

There were folks who would caution us to keep our bedroom private and not share it with anyone, but we were not comfortable with that advice. In my heart, I knew God was testing us, and we trusted that He would provide better accommodations for us and the saints, or anyone else in need.

My husband and I have always had a good relationship. We understand each other to such a degree that with a glance, we are able to communicate. When he would come home with someone for an impromptu meeting, brunch, dinner, or even to sleep over, the welcome mat was always out.

I grew up in a home where we were taught how to welcome strangers, so the same principle was carried over into my matrimonial home.

My father was the organist in the church. My siblings had good voices to harmonize and we were always practicing songs to sing at young people's meetings. This was a part of how we would welcome our guests.

When I think of the goodness of Jesus
and all He has done for me
My soul cries out Hallelujah
Thank God for saving me
&
How beautiful heaven must be
Sweet home of the happy and free
Fair haven of rest for the weary
How beautiful heaven must be.
&
It's joy, unspeakable and full of glory
Full of glory, full of glory
It's joy, unspeakable and full of glory
The half has never yet been told.

These songs were always greatly accepted and the unusual presentation welcomed.

I truly believe in sharing and caring, especially on the mission field, to help the less fortunate in a tangible way. It is good for me to roll back the curtains to see how far He has brought me. He has helped both of us to always reach out to the saints, no matter what their needs were.

Many of us soon forget where we were before the Lord took us in. We behave now as if we were born wealthy and have always been able to afford whatever we need. Let us remember that the bread we cast upon the waters today will return after many days. It's up to us to decide the type of bread we cast.

Will you be able to look on your bread when it comes back to you?

Rung 38: Esther

Elizabeth was still an only child, and I was looking forward to an addition – someone she could share with. When I became pregnant with Esther, Elizabeth was six years old. She was quite aware of the fact that she would soon share her room and toys with her new sibling.

As we awaited the arrival of our new addition, I kept thinking, "I must be the only one going through this discomfort." This seemed like a long and painful process that would never come to an end. I selfishly did not think of the others who had been down this road. Why should I consider myself unique?

During the time of my pregnancy, I had a frightening experience. A young man, whose mother was a member of our congregation, came to New York. He was seeking medical attention for a life-threatening disease. He attended one of our meetings, surrendered his life to the Lord, became a member of our church, and continued seeking the Lord for his healing. Many thought he would not survive. The news went back to Jamaica that he was still alive, and many came to see if this was really so.

Shortly after, the sickness intensified and he was diagnosed as demented. A few days later, his condition worsened. He was taken to Kings County Hospital for observation and was then admitted.

I was busy doing my daily chores one morning when at about eleven o'clock, the doorbell rang. Looking through the peephole, I saw the young man standing there. I opened the door. He walked right past me without saying a word and made his way to the kitchen. Even though I was frightened, I was familiar with his condition and could not turn him away. I offered him lunch and questioned him about his physical and mental state. After a rather extensive one-way conversation, I became weary and, leaving him there, I went to take a nap.

About ten minutes later, I had dozed off when the slight movement of the bed woke me. I became aware of the young man stretched out beside me. I froze. Should I get up? Not knowing what to do, I continued to feign sleep. I didn't know if he was just tired or getting ready to attack me. After a few minutes, I was able to discreetly maneuver a call to a friend. She advised me to wait until I was sure that he was asleep, and then vacate the room. As soon as I could, I notified my husband and told him of the situation. He told me to stay calm; he would be home as soon as possible. I did just that.

Later that evening, all four of us sat down to dinner. As Cecil interrogated the young man about his earlier behavior, the doorbell rang.

"I'll get it!" Cecil said sternly and walked towards the door. A few minutes passed, and he was still at the door. I could hear voices in the hallway and tried to listen to what it was all about.

There were at least twelve New York City police officers, with their guns drawn, batons in hand, and handcuffs ready. The hospital had notified them that a demented man was on the loose. His family had also been contacted. They informed the hospital that the only place he could have gone was his pastor's house.

The trauma from this experience almost sent me into labor. Anxiety almost got the better of me, but quickly I regained my composure and was able to cope. I thank God that Cecil was able to appease the officers, although they were still determined to use the handcuffs. In the end, Compassion was shown in a remarkable way. Just when things looked hopeless, God delivered again. Because of my husband's reputation as the pastor of a church in the community, the situation was dealt with, with much respect.

The result of this incident, in which we experienced the healing hands of God, is one of victory and celebration for the life of this young man. His distraught relatives praised Jesus in thanksgiving and adoration for His divine intervention.

I continued to wait for our baby doing as my doctor advised and whatever else it took to have a safe delivery. The complications were many, but the days were shorter.

It was late that Saturday night on September 8, 1984. Cecil was at a banquet in the Bronx. Before he left, he leaned over with a kiss and soberly asked me not to have the baby before his return. Half an hour before Cecil came home, a painful feeling swept over me. I told myself that it was nothing and went back to sleep. But as soon as Cecil retired for bed, the pain returned. I kept quiet until it became unbearable. With a nudge, I told him it was time. He thought I was joking, but Esther was not. She was ready!

Methodist Hospital was only fifteen minutes away, but with the pain, it seemed further. It was about midnight when we arrived at the registration desk. As usual, Cecil got excited because of the lengthy admittance procedure. Finally, I was taken to the labor room. The delivery was not peaches and cream, as it had been with Elizabeth. All the songs and scripture verses I knew vanished from my thoughts and were quickly replaced with screams and shouts.

The ordeal began with much pain, and pushing, and pain, and more pushing. I was trying to work with Dr. Bursacks, but the more I pushed, the more helpless he seemed. I knew that I was in trouble when he looked at me, wiped his sweaty brow, and walked away without saying a word.

My husband was still standing there, and I saw fear in his eyes when he bent down and whispered that he loved me. He said that I should try again. With tears, I replied, "I love you, too." It was at this point that I managed to gather all the strength I had left, and then tightly closed my eyes and made one more attempt to push this new life into the world.

Finally, it was all over. Cecil gave a sigh of relief as the smile on his face spread to mine.

Esther weighed eight pounds and two ounces and looked exactly like me. Cecil counted all ten fingers and toes, checking to see if she had any birth defects, but she was a perfect child.

When Elizabeth was born, she had looked so much like her father that we nicknamed her "Little Cecil."

Although Esther looked a lot like me, she was still Esther.

It was Sunday morning, and Cecil made calls to our church with the news of our new baby. A long-standing friend was asked to bring the sermon, while Cecil kept us company.

Two weeks after Esther's birth, Dr. Wilfred A. Shaw, Cecil's spiritual mentor and father in the gospel, urgently requested him to conduct a week of revival meetings in Jamaica, beginning in a few days. He could have declined the invitation with the excuse of the birth of his new daughter Esther, but instead, he accepted and began making plans to attend.

Answering a Macedonian call has never been a question for us, for "*where duty calls or danger, be never wanting there.*"

Rung 39: Being Careful

*S*ince the birth of our children, it has never been a problem as to whether we could fulfill our mission obligations because of not being able to find a babysitter, nor were there any setbacks due to illness. It was an established fact that they were a part of the team. I believe that is where family worship began. We were able to instill God in our children, have regular devotions, and keep them pointed in the right direction. The Bible teaches:

> *Train up a child in the way he should go:*
> *and when he is old, he will not depart from it.*
> (Proverbs 22:6)

I know that it's not the easiest job to go on the mission field with children. However, Cecil and I decided that they would be a part of the team until they were old enough to make their own choice about whether or not they were called for this part of the ministry. Eventually the time came when Esther began making decisions on her own. We were conducting a gospel crusade in Jamaica and had already made travel arrangements including all three of us. Elizabeth had to be in school and could not attend the convention in St. Vincent and the Grenadines.

While in Jamaica, we experienced a few major deficiencies, such as power outages and water shortages. Esther's declaration was that she would not be going to St. Vincent and the Grenadines as previously planned, as the mission field was not for her at this time. This was her first major decision. It didn't matter that she had never been there. She thought that the conditions would be the same there as in Jamaica.

The mission field is not a vacation spot; it is a battleground. We faced all sorts of demons and were compelled to cast them out in the name of Jesus. In each service, the power of God was always felt and demonstrated. The sick were healed, backsliders returned, believers strengthened, and souls led to Christ. We saw the magnitude of our commitment during these services, but solely trusted in God.

Hundreds of others called to ministry have lost the vision because they no longer see a serious need for seeking God's presence in their services. It is in these situations that we should be most alert; staying in constant communication with what the Spirit has to say.

I have been in crusade meetings where demons spoke through individuals and have listened to strange voices manifested most fervently.

During one of our crusades, an experience occurred in a village called Nine Turns in Clarendon, Jamaica. The Spirit of God revealed the workings of Satan as my husband belted out the word under much anointing. The manifestation of witchcraft spirits lined the choir seats and the podium. There were rumors that satanic devices were buried under the pulpit and in the organ. The Holy Spirit revealed this through the servant of God that night and, in no uncertain terms, the devil's strongholds were torn down. The pastor's wife was set free from the hands of Satan, who had oppressed her for many years. For those of us who have overcome the wicked one, let us spread the gospel of Jesus and His love, as time is of the essence.

When we leave on a mission, it is strongly recommended that each one on the team "be filled with the Holy Spirit," with the evidence of speaking in tongues "as the Spirit gives utterance." One of the main purposes is that when a demon is cast out, it has to find a body in which to manifest; if a member of the team is not filled with the precious Holy Spirit, they become susceptible to the demon's use. This will certainly create additional work for us.

It is always necessary and of the utmost importance that we remain in one accord with a true heart to worship, constantly on the alert so that if we were called upon to dismiss the spirit of opposition and division from any angle, we would be ready.

Getting on each other's nerves during crusade was common; the enemy uses every device to divide and conquer. He sometimes brings humiliation and aggressive behavior so that we will lose focus.

Sometimes, the real person is manifested among us, and we turn the guns on one another instead of the enemy. We forget the mission and what we aim to accomplish.

We have saints who were not able to go on a mission physically with the gospel as some of us did, they stayed in the background and supported us with their prayers and finances.

As the pastor's wife, I have noticed many believers that have hung back; they are not interested in reaching souls or giving of their substance. Replacement is easy because there are others who are ready, willing, and able. God wants willing and submissive vessels, so let us be Christians and "care for the dying, snatch them in pity from sin and the grave."

They that worship Him must worship Him in spirit and in truth. (John 4:24)

God wants us to be team players – faithful, undaunted, and consistent so that we can bring out quality work. His desire is for us to be sensitive to His command; in doing so, we will reap the good of the land. All that He has is promised to us, not only in this life, but also in the life to come. The cattle on a thousand hills are His, and because we are heirs and joint-heirs with Christ, they are equally ours.

My desire has always been to extend myself to those in need and to give all credit to Him. God will share all that He has, except His glory. He will not share His praise. He will not share His worship. God is a jealous God. Let us work on where we have fallen short and strive for the mark.

Let us not be desirous of the lifting up of ourselves. If we are not recognized for our work, we should not be murmuring; the Lord will reward us in due time. There are some believers who like to be applauded. If they are not thanked, or elevated in praise, they create havoc. I believe it is a form of flattery. If leaders always have to do this in order to keep them in the church, we are in trouble.

There is always a spate of intensifying jealousy when one is mentioned more than the other, therefore, it is wise to leave this well enough alone, and keep the peace! Let the wheat and tare be until the day of harvest.

If we change our focus and just respect each other, by giving a word of encouragement and a prayer and by taking self out of the picture, it will be the greatest battle that was ever fought. Let us yield to God and submit to be renewed in holiness.

At the inception of our church, I was the cleaning lady, and Cecil was the janitor on call. None of us could be lifted up in pride. It was just us. This was not the most attractive job, but it came with the package – this is my husband's favorite saying. We would not worship in an unclean sanctuary; therefore, we both had to clean it. We saw this as a part of the ministry and it was okay. We continued doing so until help came.

In time past, parishioners took pleasure in cleaning the church, and you dared not offer anyone a dime. It would be an insult. Now, most churches have to compensate persons doing this job. One of the first things that they query is how much are they going to be paid, especially if they have to do it all day. It is difficult to find someone who will gladly do church chores without expecting something in return.

My prayer is that this will not be named among us. Others have complained of this behavior in their assembly, and are somewhat displeased. Cecil honestly believes that if an individual is unemployed, and is asked to do a particular job at the church, it is up to him or the finance committee whether or not to reward the individual based on their financial standing.

Some believers are not always able to pay their tithes and offerings, due to a lack of funds, yet they refuse to give even their time. The sharing and giving of a believer's time and talent has become a rare commodity. Many want to feel satisfied by receiving a reward now and the unearned balance in the "sweet bye and bye." The late Bishop Dr. Wilfred A. Shaw's once said, "Give God some raw material to work with."

Give of your best to the Master
Give of the strength of your youth
Throw your soul's fresh, glowing ardor
Into the battle for truth.
Jesus has set the example.
Dauntless was he, young and brave

Give Him your loyal devotion
Give Him the best that you have.

As we further our strides, I realize that rungs like these are not the easiest to climb.

I had to make sure that I was setting the example of the things that we taught in prayer meetings and Bible studies, where so many people were looking to us to hear what He was saying through His Word. A lot of times, the Holy Spirit confirmed that the revelation I got to communicate, in word or song, was done at the right time.

Frequently, I make comments like, "I honestly believe that I was called to sing, not to preach or to teach," but in whatever I do when I stand before a congregation or any audience, I need God's anointing so that yokes will be broken.

Be careful when we are called upon to impart to others; let it be as streams flowing over the Rock, "Christ Jesus" who is the fountain of life. Today, many are not striving to know more about Jesus and His Word, and we suffer from spiritual insufficiency, which is quite noticeable when one stands to speak. The "not prepared" comments should be omitted from the vocabulary of the Christian; we should be so built up and established from eating and drinking from the resources of the Word of God, that at any time we are called to testify, there is a Word.

Whenever a leader is not equipped, their congregation suffers and there will likely be no growth. Hear me, children of God: Never sit under lazy leadership or you will die spiritually, unless you do something for yourself.

More about Jesus I would know
More of His grace to others show
More of His saving fullness see
More of His love who died for me.

More about Jesus let me learn
More of His Holy will discern
Spirit of God my teacher be,
Showing the things of Christ to me.

Rung 40: Make No Mistake

During the first year of our ministry, there were some who thought their spiritual insight was better than that of the pastor. The spirit of

Jezebel tried sneaking in a few times, but God exposed the spirit and disqualified the attack.

How did He reveal the Jezebel spirit? He exposed the subtle command that he presented, the insubordination that went uncorrected, along with the determination to be recognized, as well as the strong desire to control. My responsibilities at the church went well at first, and then all of a sudden I was not competent, and complaints went flying left, right, and center. The spirit wedged himself between the few helpers we had, trying to make a better showing, and presenting an awesome magnetic desire for his services. An all-sufficient authority was now posted in the midst of our small administration and began working against the set-up that my husband had put in place.

Many times we underestimate the power of God and what He says in His Word. It is good to have the gift of discernment. If He says it, we need not query, doubt, or wonder if it will happen. The Word of God will never return void.

The Holy Spirit is not the author of confusion. I believe that if a thing is revealed, it is because the Holy Spirit is capable of rationalizing it with care.

For me to find a genuine friend was a rare commodity; some relationships were not genuine even when they appeared to be. The hidden agendas could not be concealed anymore. I was not oblivious to the enemy's devices, but I kept my awareness hidden as I was committed to the work of the Lord.

In conversation with God, I would ask Him if this was really how Christians ought to behave when the lives of men and women are at risk. God told me to pray for them that they will find true repentance and acknowledge their transgression without hypocrisy.

To be honest, I was never a friendly person. "Hello" was the only word I ever wanted to say. I never sought to be close to anyone because the friends I chose had already proven untrue.

At the beginning, I never asked God to direct me to my acquaintances, and comments were made such as, "I like the pastor, but there is something about his wife that my spirit can't take." Most of the time, they were right.

My spirit was on target with their behavior, especially when they pretended to be under the influence of the Holy Spirit. A person who does wrong on remote doesn't realize that they remain in partial blindness as far as sin is concerned; nothing such a person does is sincere or honest. When they are reprimanded, they simply do the same thing over and over again. The assembly is loaded with great pretenders without moral attributes or class.

The eyes of God go to and fro. He is my eyes, ears, and feet. My aim is to stay under His watchful eye. Nothing occurs without the Holy Spirit knowing about it, especially when it is personal or deals with my family. I have been born again long enough, and I am not ignorant of the enemy's devices.

When I enter the sanctuary, the Holy Spirit places me on high alert, on "code red." When so many different spirits meet, it is hell if I am not prayed up. Demons would be hanging on to me from every angle, with a determination to capture my sanity, but I can depend on the Holy Spirit to deflect them. I refuse to allow the enemy to overcome me, especially when I know that greater is He that is in me than he that is in the world.

When you are called of God, the fiery darts will never penetrate. I have gone through challenging times, and sometimes, I would like to crawl up under a juniper tree and die, especially when my faith is challenged and I am at my lowest ebb.

That's what a Jezebel-spirit wants – for me to release my confidence to him so that he can have dominion. When he does not have dominion, he is like a pit bull on drugs. I have experienced this firsthand. He puts his satanic influence into action through unrelenting vigilance and is determined to let nothing stand in his way. The Jezebel-spirit is not necessarily labeled a woman; men, too, can be such a spirit.

Again I thank God for the gift of a quiet and meek spirit. He taught me how to watch and pray. You cannot be a child of God and never see the enemy in operation.

My constant prayer is to maintain this gift of discernment.

Smith Wigglesworth was asked, "How long do you pray when you pray?" His reply was, "Ten minutes! But I do not go ten minutes without praying." Prayer changes things. Prayer will bring your enemy to his knees. Prayer will fix things. Whatever it is, give it to Jesus. In my secret prayer closet, I commune with God as "friend to friend." He is my trusted one! I tell Him everything.

Are you weary, are you heavy hearted
Tell it to Jesus, Tell it to Jesus
Are you grieving over joys departed
Tell it to Jesus alone.

Tell it to Jesus, tell it to Jesus
He's a friend that's well known
You have no other such a friend or brother
Tell it to Jesus alone.

There is always a force to reckon with as soon as one decides to take a stance. The evil that lurks in some believers' hearts is vigilant. The enemy knows that he can use costly mistakes to steal our blessings, and if we are not careful, we go along life's pathway dwelling on our mistakes, our disappointments, and our failures.

It's a pleasure for us to share family time with some of our congregants who have no immediate relatives except for the saints. They really need more than just a "God bless you" or a shoulder to lean on. They need to know from time to time that someone cares about their well-being. You can tell those who really desire special attention, while with others, just a touch is enough. I believe that God admires this.

Believers can be easily swayed if they are not taught the importance of showing love through giving. They will become unkind, selfish, and less sympathetic, and this could cause them to withdraw instead of huddling together as one in Christ to fulfill the mission.

I was almost influenced at one time not to go beyond the 10-percent commitment. I nearly lost my joy, my testimony, and my song. I had to speak to my soul:

It is not in my own approval that I share,
but to allow the Spirit of God to do His will.

All to Jesus O surrender, all to Him I freely give
I will ever love and trust Him, in His presence daily live

All to Jesus I surrender, Lord I give myself to thee
Fill me with thy love and power; let thy blessing fall on me

Chapter 8

MY SHOES

Rung 41: Pious and Good

*R*emember the Cinderella story? This fairy tale had a lot of spiritual morals. I recall how we would sit and read fairy tales as children. The first tale we asked mom to read was that of Cinderella. Of the entire tale, I can specifically remember reading the words that her mother spoke to her before she died, "My dear child, be pious and good."

Some would ask, what is a fairy? A fairy is "a tiny mythical being with human form and superhuman powers." A tale is "a brief story, true or fictitious; gossip, a lie."

In Christendom, I would like to think differently, yet I often feel like Cinderella as I work tirelessly within the ministry and sometimes reap much hurt and betrayal. There are some believers who despise others because they are blessed, forgetting that God elevates whoever He chooses to a place of wealth and independence.

I am not trying to rewrite the Cinderella story, but I have to make mention of her stepsisters, the wicked stepmother, and their tragic end. Does this story give you any kind of picture of the consequences that those with evil hearts face? So I say, "Be good and pious."

It is evident that Cinderella was the very stone that everyone had refused. Yet she became the cornerstone of a kingdom. In the fullness of time came her blessing in the midst of her rigorous chores. She waited patiently as she knew her golden opportunity would soon arrive. Many times we look at someone and presume him or her to be good. However, to be pious prepares us to somewhat accept the fact that religion is not the answer, but God is.

Whenever the New Year dawns, many people make plans to turn over a new leaf by making a New Year's resolution to change things in their lives. Some often think that this will make them a good candidate for heaven or that it will make them a Christian. It is good to be good, but it must be from the heart. It's an inside job.

In the tale of Cinderella, obedience was the key that unlocked her future. If she had not done as her mother had asked, her future would have been different.

The Scriptures declare, "*If we be willing and obedient, we shall eat the good of the land.*" Some of the morals here are geared towards what I have been sharing.

Please enjoy this rung. But before I can move on from sharing, I would like to remind you of a good and pious person's attributes. What does it mean to be a good person? Here are a few definitions: *good* means "efficient; beneficial; unspoiled; valid; healthy; sound; worthy; happy;

pious; of favorable quality; proper; genuine; pleasant; ample." The concordance refers to *good* as "kind, excellent, fit." When you are referred to as a good person, then you are all of the above.

And God is able to make all grace abound toward you,
That ye, always having all sufficiency in all things,
May abound to every good work.
(2 Corinthians 9:8)

I am sure that every person knows whether or not he or she is a good person within himself or herself. When the enemy presents thoughts of evil, what matters is how those thoughts are handled. Let's break this down. An evil thought comes to mind, so how do we choose to handle that thought? A person with good morals should be able to dismiss an evil thought. When acted upon, an evil thought can cost you your life and the lives of others, and your freedom and the freedom of others.

I had many choices when I migrated to New York. There were forces, both good and bad, that could either make or break me. I remember riding the train from Brooklyn to Manhattan in the early seventies. Young people would ride between cars and smoke and hang out, sometimes getting into fights and doing all kinds of dangerous acrobatics.

The devil tempted me with smoking, making it seem like everyone else was smoking and that I was the only one who was not! He whispered to me that it was okay, that it was only a cigarette, and there was nothing wrong in trying it once.

I was a young girl, but not a young Christian. I was brought up in a Christian home and had temptations to do wrong things. The devil has no respect for me. He could care less about my background. My mother's admonishment when I left our home in Jamaica was, "Be careful now, Eleanor. You don't have me to watch over you. Keep saved, keep well. God bless you." Like Cinderella's mother's words, "Be good and pious," I feel a lump in my throat every time I remember my mother's words. I thank God that she is still alive and that her words did not fall on deaf ears. I love you, Mom!

Mother always believed that her children would grow up to be the best in society – the next president of the United States, the world's greatest heart surgeon, or something even greater to make her and my father proud. Today, we have mothers who wish evil on their children, which results from a bad past. They believe that their children will not amount to anything.

A good affirmation can change a child's future, even if their parents have suffered a bad past. I do not know what the past of Cinderella's mother entailed, but she certainly wished only good for her daughter. Although Cinderella was treated horribly, she was obedient, and in the end, received the better of the deal.

We know that the tale of Cinderella is a fictitious one, but it falls close to reality – today, an individual that we believe to be less fortunate can be treated similarly if he or she falls into the wrong hands. Although I was not treated like Cinderella, I loved her humbleness and obedience, and the lesson that her fictitious tale taught me. It reaffirmed that my future lies in the hands not of a man who has no idea of the worn rungs, but in the hands of Jesus Christ, a man who continues to create new rungs. This is really something to shout about.

Men as a whole have not had the problems that women often have. May I remind you, it's about my shoes! Sometimes the discomfort arises from just a few believers who have caused my shoes to be a bit uncomfortable. But they are my shoes, and my desire is that I be allowed to walk in them. Even if I accidentally lose or misplace them, they are still mine. Of course, nothing takes the place of a shoe that is designed for you. Do not judge a man until you have walked in his shoes: the contours will surely be different, but at least you will get a feel of what it is like to be him. One might admire the shoes of another person in a good way, but sometimes people are simply envious of the type of shoes you are wearing. So instead of making a genuine compliment, they think: "Those should be mine."

But in all of this, let us demonstrate what we stand for. Let us be the friend of the friendless, the friend in need and in deed, and even more so, the friend that sticks closer than a brother. It is good to be important, but it is more important to be good.

A model is usually one of a kind, and one that stands out to be looked at, who sends a commanding message to the eyes. We do profit from our own example, and we can know from other people's reactions whether it is good or bad.

I cannot predict how far I will walk in my shoes, but I am given the ability to endure to the end, and to effectively communicate and share my thoughts and feelings with the saints. I find it very awkward to be a blessing if I try to operate outside of my character. The self-confidence and the ability to be effective must come from the true me, in order that I may be able to stay in leadership.

If I am both pious and good, there is nothing wrong with my stepping out in confidence and sharing my knowledge with others. Someone once said, "I would rather be whipped than start, but two minutes before I finish, I would rather be shot than stop." I've started many years now, and the benefits I am receiving are awesome. You, too, can reap so much from this prescription, so please try your best to catch on.

If I were not a good person already, I would now begin to become one. This journey begins with just a step, and the first step is to the college of learning how to pray. When I pray, I get results. Kneeling in prayer, or prostrate before Him in adoration and intercessory prayer, thanking Him for His goodness and mercies, or even complaining about the hurts I suffered, but with a trusting heart, I have always had good results. I know that my God cares, and that He shall supply all of my needs according to His riches in glory.

Leaders are supposed to lead by example. The enemy knows this and so he will stop at nothing until he gets that leader to make a fool of himself, even if he has to use those closest to them to do so. I was always a prime target for the enemy, so I ran for cover constantly. Jesus is my refuge and my fortress.

Hide me under the blood Lord, hide me under the blood
Hide me under the blood Lord, hide me under the blood
Hide me under the blood Lord, hide me under the blood
And I shall be satisfied.

Let me see thy face Lord, let me see thy face
Let me see thy face Lord, let me see thy face
Let me see thy face Lord, let me see thy face
And I shall be satisfied.

Rung 42: If the Shoe Fits

Someone once said that one of the beautiful traits about me is that I am a woman who wears many hats. Then they proceeded to describe all my responsibilities and the capacities in which I served. Not only do my shoes fit in these capacities, but they are quite comfortable. Many committees in churches find it difficult to discuss anything that has to do with the First Lady. This is always a highly-flammable subject. Why? The shoes!

Bob Marley's suggestion comes in handy: "If the cap fits, wear it." So, if the shoe fits, wear it. But what if it doesn't? Quit. Do not even try to walk in it because everyone will see the blood dripping from the self-inflicted wound made in order to make the slipper fit, as Cinderella's sisters found out. The Prince of Peace should be taking you home after the party is over. Will He refuse you until you have found repentance? He will be returning for a church without spot or wrinkle.

Cinderella's wicked stepmother told her stepdaughters to cut off their toes and heels in order to fit into a shoe that did not belong to either of them. She told them that when they became queen, they would have no more need for their feet, and they believed her. What have we done to our feet in order to wear someone else's shoes?

The foot is one of the most important parts of our body. Of course, we can get by without it physically, but we need it spiritually – we need every part in order to fully be a part of the body of Christ. Have we cut off loving our neighbor as ourselves? Have we cut off the joy of the Lord? Have we cut off the happiness and trust we once knew? Have we cut off true friendship and confidentiality?

The enemy will tell us we have no need of them. Let us be careful of inflecting ourselves for something that only brings a moment of joy. There are a lot of lessons that we can learn from this tale.

It is best for us to find our proper fit and be content. Let us not try to be in someone else's place, unless is to help in a positive way. We all have our duties to perform and were created to serve in our own capacity without any mystification. God made us uniquely different. He put His mind in us. Remember! We have the mind of Christ.

God has given us a proper fit and He never makes a mistake. If He wanted us all to do the same chores, He would have made us alike. Even our fingerprints are different. Identical twins look alike, but something is different about them. Our feet are unique – they determine our destiny, our path, and how we use them. We have been to cemeteries and seen the writings on the tombstones. The dashes between those years symbolize the shoes worn. From birth and until our demise, God maps out the path that we take. He knows where our footsteps go because He orders them.

I am not envious of anyone else's shoes. I have my own custom-made pair, which can only be worn by me. I have never had a streak of envy for anything that anyone had. To God be the glory! It is very important that I concentrate on my own whereabouts and what I do with my time.

Whatever is not mine is left alone. Envy will forever exist among believers. Another believer's life will always look appealing to the envious eye. It will be very enticing. Evil and demonic spirits will keep whispering, "That life looks better than mine. I should be the one. It should be me. That should be mine." This continues to surface among us every day.

Barriers are placed before me and walls are raised against me regularly. Prejudice and pride have stared me in the face. I have been told outright, "You cannot go there. It is a prestigious affair and they do not cater to people like you." This is one of the things that Satan and his imps are telling Christians today. Satan is showing us the filthy rags that he wants us to keep wearing so that we will not come into the fullness of God our Father. Until we walk into the knowledge of God and fully understand what it is that He wants us to do, we will keep spinning as if we have no direction. I made up my mind to step away from the shoe store, which I call the outer court. I am not even accepting the Holy Place, but will go beyond the veil to be in the presence of a Holy God. The Scriptures say: "*For envy they killed Jesus.*"

> *Therefore when they were gathered together, Pilate said unto them, Whom will ye that I release unto you? Barabbas, or Jesus which is called Christ? For he knew that for envy they had delivered him.* (Matthew 27:17-18)

Envy will always be widespread among us, causing much uproar in our homes and churches. I believe that one of the reasons why churches are desolate and homes are falling apart is because somebody was not paying attention to their own spiritual responsibility.

One of the tricks that the enemy uses in churches today is distraction. Christians are not longing for worship any more. Their attention is turned to other things – things that are so intense and wicked that they allow the enemy to enter into their hearts, and they would send their brother or sister to the front of the battle to be slain in order to fulfill some wish of their own, and they have no remorse. They will cry at the funeral and make open confessions about how this believer was their best friend. Yeah right! Come hell or high water they will divide and conquer, forgetting completely that they should be real saints without envy, or murderous intention, and be sanctified and filled with the Holy Spirit.

There are many other distractions that exist in our church environment today. Some of them are beyond belief. The thought of rehashing them makes me feel dirty. There are some things that should not be named among us. That is why the Lord has instructed me to relinquish any spirit that is in opposition to His will and purpose for my life.

I was never a person to pattern myself after anyone else. I try to remain in the key of B-natural. In the past, the enemy wanted me to believe that I had no potential. I knew that I had issues that needed working on. As it stands today, I refuse to walk in someone else's shoes for fear of developing spiritual *Morton's neuroma*.

Enoch walked with God and he was not, for God took him. Elijah walked with God, and he too went up from the presence of Elisha. God ordered the footsteps of these men. They went wherever God wanted them to go, and He directed their paths.

It is sad to say that many people today are sometimes walking the path under duress because they are wearing the shoes that the enemy has provided for them. This gives his enemy the right to be in the driver's seat. He manipulates you by making you forget where you are going, and your calling and destiny.

I have come to realize that I will not receive my full benefits from God if I seek my own path. It is like working for a company where you are placed on probation for a period. During this time, you are observed, watched, and scrutinized. If you fail during this period, not only will you not receive the promised benefits, but you will be terminated as well. You are on a probationary period now. So run with comfortable shoes, keep up the pace of your praise, your worship, and your songs. More than all strive to be true worshippers.

If you find yourself wearing anything that is not yours, maybe you are uncomfortable, like David. Perhaps the problem is your shoes? They may be causing blisters or sores! It's time to take them off and ask God for your right size.

There will be some people with ugly motives still trying to discourage you from relieving yourself of the burden, but continue to remember who you are and keep working on your dreams.

I wear my shoes with dignity, loyalty, uprightness, and pride. The cushion that I rest on mentally, emotionally, and most of all, spiritually, is the Holy Spirit who makes sure I am comfortable.

Over the years, I have seen leaders of various churches trying to fit into others' shoes. What's so wrong with your own? Sometimes they try to pattern an individual so much that it goes from the ridiculous to the sublime, and I am sure this stands out clearly in the eyes of the congregation. It is disheartening to see the membership getting frustrated to the point where they begin to decline, and then the congregation that was once vibrant both spiritually and mentally loses its strength in a short time, especially if the leader proves to be an impostor. I have visited churches where it is hard to tell if the church is edified from their performance. I often comment, "God must really have a hard time getting them to pay Him some attention." They are too busy in the fitting room, trying to make it work.

Let us be ourselves. The shoes we wear should be worn with reverential fear. When you are tempted otherwise, please remember this prayer.

Today, I lose myself to the Holy Spirit
and to walk in the fullness of Your purpose
for my life. I know that I am capable of doing
much more in You than I allow to happen.
Therefore, I lose my spirit, soul, and body
to be totally yours today! Amen.
Adapted: John Paul Jackson

Rung 43: I Refuse To Take Off My Shoes

At this point, I really would like to get a little personal and kind of let my hair down with you, and open up some of my heart's secrets. I believe that this will help all of us who wear different shoes. Those not wearing their own shoes will always have a fear of losing them, and that's where zealousness and envy get acquainted. Becoming friends, they walk hand in hand. Pretending to be another, whatever the reason, is a dangerous thing. When one is called from sin to grace, there are some positive, noticeable changes in the behavioral pattern that you can't miss. I have seen people who cannot feel comfortable unless they are doing something against the teachings of the Holy Word; they are always sneaking around, as if they are hiding something when they have absolutely no reason to.

The worst part about it is that there is no rhyme or reason for such behavior.

Stand fast therefore in the liberty wherewith Christ hath made us
free, and be not entangled again with the yoke of bondage.
(Galatians 5:1)

If you love yourself – I mean really love yourself – look in the mirror and say to the person looking back at you: "Hey, I love you, you are special." Please do not have the desire to be someone else. Stay as I say in the key of B-natural.

During the period that Cecil and I were courting, he bought me a record. Some of you are not familiar with courting. During my time, "courting" meant getting to know each other better in an uncontaminated atmosphere before marriage. Now, no one has that time. This is one of the reasons why the divorce rate is so high. Everyone wants a quick fix.

CDs were not as popular back then as they are now. We had LPs and forty-fives. Cecil bought me an LP with the Commodore's song, "Three Times a Lady," which included the song ". . . and I love you." That was all good and well, but I did not wait for him to tell me that he loved me before I started loving myself. He did not tell me who I was before I knew myself. I knew that I had a high self-esteem and was destined for greatness. It is not the title of First Lady that made me who I am. Sure enough, it helped to enhance my demeanor and kept me conscious when I was in a civic setting. More than that, I am an example representing both God and my husband.

As First Lady of a very active, dynamic, and fast-growing ministry, I have been in situations where I was put under scrutiny, but as a woman of God I was not fearful, for the curious eye could not see me because my life is hid with Christ in God. In the meantime, I stayed focused in my place and tried not to cause anyone to stumble. My position is one that is easily coveted because it looks prestigious. Let me help somebody here. It is only in appearance! But it's a constant battle. This position has taught me how to fight warfare daily, not only for the salvation of my own soul, but also for my husband so that he will continue fulfilling the call. I have to deal with false spirits on a regular basis, but I thank God for them. They keep me on my knees.

Who I am is a gift from God. He saw me and knew me from the time I was in my mother's belly, and He predestined me to higher heights. When the Lord joined Cecil and me, we became one. We found buried treasures in each other and decided that we were going to accentuate the positive, and forget about the negative. He had my love and I had his.

Sporadic clouds form over our lives, but God puts a rainbow with them each time. Sometimes I thought that our marriage would dissipate, but we continue to remind each other of the vows that we made between us and God. The friends that I sometimes looked to for words of advice and consolation were the very ones that betrayed my trust. They were great pretenders who invaded our privacy, and wore sheep's clothing, but the Holy Spirit unmasked them and the blood of Jesus prevailed.

The blood prevails, the blood of the risen Lord,
Power to save just like in olden days
The blood prevails no matter what others say
Thank God, the blood prevails.

There were times when Cecil came home, and the responsibility of the church seemed at bit heavy; it was a lot to deal with every now and again. Some of the weight got shifted to my shoulders, so I shared the heaviness with him.

Once I seriously asked him, "What did the enemy do today? What happened between here and there? When you left home today, you were in good spirits. We shared some jokes, laughed, kissed, and then said goodbye. What went wrong during the time you were out?"

He replied, "You are the closest to me so you will feel the brunt of my work. Sorry, *this comes with the package.*" Those words were always his answer, especially during heated discussions.

And of course the devil spoke to me immediately, saying, "Walk away. You will be better off without this." Believe it or not, it took me two days to recognize that this was the devil speaking. However, regardless of the prevailing circumstances, I stood my ground.

I refused to succumb to the enemy and his devices although there were times that I felt that I could not go one step further.

Sometimes I feel I cannot go one step farther on,
My body waxing older and faltering steps begun,
But when I think of Jesus and what He's done for me.
Then I cry, to the Rock of Ages, hide Thou me.

Oh Rock of Ages, hide Thou me,
There is no other refuge that can save but Thee
Through this whole world I wander so far, far from Thee
Then I cry, to the Rock of Ages, hide Thou me.

In the midst of my struggles, I continued to hold to God's unchanging hand. He had my back, so I could hold my peace even in times when I would have been justified to unleash my anger or other strong emotion. I kept a calm spirit. If I say that I was not alarmed, I would not be truthful, but I had a prayer deep within that kept me.

I could have abandoned my shoes, kicking them off and saying the hell with it. The devil desired for me to become violent and unruly. He had no respect for me and, believe me, the feeling is mutual. As the strong arm of God was holding me, I could not let go. God knows my strengths and weaknesses, so when I was weak He carried me. I thought sometimes, when the weight was so obvious on my brow, that I had been left alone, but He made a way.

At times, I knew that I could not hide the frown even when I tried, and despite the enemy's devices, I still have to give greetings with a, "God bless you." This may appear hypocritical, but I believe it was diplomacy. When I'm greeted with a smile that masks another face altogether, in spite of the callousness of the person, I pray that they will have a renewed heart. My prayer is always for the double-minded man, who is unstable in his ways, to turn and pant for the living bread.

There were times when the Holy Spirit would show me things, not for me to retaliate but just to bring me to a place of maturity and awareness. May be to see how I would handle it. When I feel the forces of evil, I just know that I am kept covered and the blood of Jesus triumph.

My friendship and fellowship with Jesus became lovelier, and I was able to deal with the pain that comes with our growth.

I learned to have patience, endurance, love, long-suffering, meekness, and self-control; there is no law against these.

From the biography of this great author, I am reminded of who Jesus is to me, which touches me deeply. May you be blessed!

What the hand is to the lute,
What the breath is to the flute,
What is fragrance to the smell?
What the spring is to the well,
What the flower is to the bee,
That is Jesus Christ to me.
What's the mother to the child?
What the guide in pathless wild?
What is oil to troubled wave?
What is ransom to the slave?
What is water to the sea?
That is Jesus Christ to me.
Arranged by: C. H. Spurgeon.

Rung 44: Wearing My Shoes Home

I am not here for any other reason but to serve. If my mission has any other motive, I would owe the Lord a huge apology from the bottom of my heart. I have a settled peace within me, knowing that I am accomplishing the commission that God gave me. Therefore, I have a more meaningful Christian life and a stronger determination for heaven. There is nothing now that can change my desire or even shake my faith in God, especially since my prayer life has increased.

A comment from Smith Wigglesworth's life teachings reads:

I always say you cannot sing victory in a minor key
and you can never have a spiritual horizon on a low note.
If your life isn't constant pitch, you will never ring
the bell of heaven.

The ministry is at the heart of how I operate; I have no hidden motives or agendas. We are in the last days and have to make our "calling and election sure."

Whatever I do has to reflect my God-given attributes. When God placed me as one of the leaders in our church, it was permanent. My position in this organization, the church of God, is not like serving in a political realm in which there are term limits, nor is it one to allow for voting in or out. This is a kingdom call! My aim is to be a watchman and a prayer-warrior, not giving entrance to the enemy who goes about with unrelenting vigilance. As a true soldier, I am determined to negate every plan of the enemy in order to receive my reward.

I've heard of a land that is wondrously fair,
They say that its splendor is far beyond compare,
In the place that's called Heaven my soul longs to be,
But where Jesus is, it will be Heaven for me.

Heaven for me, Heaven for me
Jesus will be what makes it Heaven for me
All its beauty and wonders I'm longing to see
But if Jesus will be, it will be Heaven for me.

It is a sad reality that out of heartless envy, some folks deem me not worthy of my own shoes. The enemy has used them to set up traps and roadblocks, and to form lies and deceits against me. When I come upon these barriers, God puts a spring in my shoes so that I can leap far beyond them. Sometimes, when I come upon one of his traps, the devil wants me to throw a pity party. For a short while, I listened to that voice, but as soon as I recognized that it was not the voice of God, I hasten to dismiss that dragon, Satan. I know who I am and whose I am."

There are some who have entered the race with a determination to endure to the end, and there are others who have entered to hinder those with a desire to make it to the finish line. Most times, the enemy uses a friend or a close associate for this type of distraction.

My buddies tell me that I should have waited
They say I'm missing a whole world of fun
But I am happy and I sing with pride
I like the Christian life.

I won't lose a friend by heeding God's call
For who is a friend who would want you to fall
Others find pleasure in things I despised
I like the Christian life.

The bottom line for me is heaven; heaven will surely be worth it all. I am encouraged to press forward because I am looking at the final result. The voice of my Savior constantly says, *"Fight on, for I will never leave you nor forsake you."* I am convinced that for every situation, God has equipped me with the proper shoes. Whether these spiritual shoes are for leaping over troops, ducking below missiles, or sliding through ambushes, my Lord is able to provide the escape plan.

Over the years, my shoes became worn and a little less comfortable. When I felt as though I could not bear the discomfort, I knew that it was time for a spiritual resizing. I learned that being a First Lady, my "shoe size" was subject to change. These changes resulted from alterations in membership or being upgraded to a subsidiary mission of singing, which I was originally called to. I have learned that each tread in my life requires another "fit-stop" in God's Shoe Store!

As a child, I was told that if I didn't take care of something old, I would never get something new. Therefore, the shoes God has given me to use must always be in immaculate condition. I do not worry about what my shoes will look like when I get to heaven. One thing I do know is that I won't have to maintain them there. I can kick off my shoes and rejoice in being home at last! I am preparing every day, and am ready and waiting for His return so I can show Him my sparkling shoes.

I see the bright lights shine
It's just about home time.
I see my father standing at the door.
This world had been a wilderness

I'm ready for deliverance
I've never been this homesick before.

The mission that God gave me has never changed. But the responsibilities have expanded. The more I knew, the more I grew; and the Lord was always ready to equip me. I cannot say that I was always ready and willing to be altered, but through my faith in His promises, I knew that God would make me over into a living testimony.

"Well done, thou good and faithful servant" are the words I want to hear at the end of my race. When I get to heaven, I want my shoes to be on display. I want everyone to comment on how, even through rough terrain, I managed to keep them clean. Then I'll say, "It's through the blood!"

Chapter 9

FROM THE SETBACK

Rung 45: A Set-up

*I*t was at this time that the Lord enlarged my territory as He did unto Jabez. The ministry was the catalyst. God had already designed the way to bring me through the challenges that lay ahead of me.

I arrived in New York in April of 1970 with a desire to continue singing and doing recordings, but was faced with many setbacks. I had no knowledge of where or how to begin, and was apprehensive about making any inquiry about studio time. At that time, my financial status would not allow me to pursue my dream. I watched as the years went by and I experienced changes and challenges that shaded my plan of recording. I was somewhat discouraged because I loved singing. I grasped every opportunity for my voice to be heard at churches, concerts, weddings, banquets, and wherever else I was asked to sing.

During my search, I was requested to be a part of a singing group named the Rainbow Gospel Singers. We did one recording with the hope that this would allow us to further ourselves in the music industry, but this was not what God had in mind for me. Prior to our call to the ministry, Cecil and I rehearsed at night for hours and hours. We jumped at every opportunity given to us to sing at functions on weekends.

Our musical background proved a good enhancement to our church. Cecil was the "all-rounder." His musical talent was showcased as he played his guitar and sang at every service. The pleasure was always mine to sing along with him, no matter what. My comment, as usual, was: "I was not called to be a preacher, but if someone woke me up in the dead of night and asked me to sing, I know that I would be able to."

As you read this book, you may be seeking and searching in the hope of accomplishing your dreams. You are trusting God, but you feel like He has forgotten you. The heavens seem like brass when your prayers are not immediately answered. But know that this is only a test! Keep reading. My story will show you that God is able to deliver you from your setbacks.

Weeping may endure for a night,
But joy cometh in the morning.
(Psalms 30:5)

God allowed the enemy to have a glimpse into my future and he saw how much of a threat I am to him and how vital I am to the Kingdom of God. The enemy's desire was to sift me as wheat and abort the vision, but God had me under His control. With all of Satan's plans, I had made up my mind: "No matter what he does, I know I will succeed." God has never failed. He has never gone back on His Word. I began reading the Bible even more, making sure that I read and knew all of His promises.

It is always good to testify about God's goodness, mercy, kindness, and everlasting love. His bountiful blessings will overtake us if we remain faithful to Him. I have not seen the future, but God who holds my future assured me that it was looking bright. We can liken this to the coming of our Lord and Savior Jesus Christ. He is not yet here, but we know that He is coming because of the promise he made.

When I came to America, I knew what my original intentions were. I held on to everything with a positive and prosperous outlook and a continued determination to fulfill my dream. But when I reflected on all that the Lord had helped me to accomplish, I was still not satisfied with the strides that I had made towards my dream. Of course, the marriage was good and the children were doing great as expected, and the church was growing by leaps and bounds. Yet I yearned to fulfill my real desire – to sing professionally for the Lord.

If you have some questions in the corners of your mind
Traces of discouragement and peace you cannot find
Reflections of your past seem to face you every day
But this one thing I do know, Jesus is the way

I know you've got mountains that you think you cannot climb
I know your skies are dark, you think the sun won't shine
In case you do not know that the word of God is true
And everything He's promised, He will do for you.
- by André & Sandra Crouch

For a child of God, every disappointment makes room for the Word to come alive and show us that He will turn it around for our good. Although I was set back for a little while, I knew the contrary waves would cease. They do not last forever. They shall and must pass over (Matthew 14: 24-31). Though troubles and difficulties disturb our duty, they must not drive us from it, and in the midst of them we must press forward. We must never allow the tempest of life nor the dangers that lurk to alarm us. My God is a very present help when we are in trouble. If He says to me, "Come," I trust Him enough to know that I will not fall.

Everything that I had experienced up to this point was only setting me up to face the *real setback*. It is good to know that my hands are in the hand of the Man who stills the water. My hands are in the hand of the Man who calms the sea. When I consider my setback, I realize that it was only going to be a testimony to the goodness of Jesus. The manifestations of the enemy do not work for any length of time as long as we are steadfast in prayer and supplication.

When I thought there was peace and safety, and that I was out of the dark and approaching dawn, I experienced a real setback. I was so badly afflicted, but still I knew that the enemy had no control over me. I underwent much discomfort and went almost beyond survival. But in my weakness, God saw that I was still one of the fittest to survive. My courage was almost gone and I was not aware of the next attack or the nature of it. I was not expecting that my immediate condition would worsen. I thank God for this experience and preparedness which gave me a cushion that really lined my spiritual back to bear the brunt.

It was September of 1992, and we were getting ready for our annual crusade to be held at the church in Jamaica. As the time approached for our travel, I began experiencing terrible pain and swelling of my legs. I ignored it because I wanted to attend the week of meetings which were always so exciting, soul-winning, and refreshing. But when the aircraft touched down in Kingston, immediately I could see that I needed medical attention. However, I managed to complete the week of meetings and return to New York. When I visited the doctor, he recommended that I be hospitalized immediately. I was admitted to Kings County Hospital, and after seventeen days of tests, there was no medical explanation for my condition. Dr. Joseph DeRose decided to do a sonogram of my kidneys, which showed that they were working normally. However, something was still wrong.

Another four days went by before the doctors decided to do a biopsy of my kidneys. After this test, the results showed that I had a rare kidney disease called Glomerular Nephritis, in which the kidneys' filters become inflamed and scarred and slowly lose their ability to remove wastes and excess water from the blood to make urine. This condition caused the swelling in my body. Along with that diagnosis, I had other complications such as the spillage of an unusually high amount of protein in my urine, and I even had hepatitis. To my advantage, my antibodies fought it in the initial stage. Dr. DeRose assured me that the hepatitis would not return – only its residue was present and that would soon disappear. But I had no sinews in my joints. On one Sunday morning, I was screened off from the other patient in the room because my blood count had gone down three times. There were many of us on the renal floor and some were closer to dying than others. There were many nights when I would fall asleep talking to my roommate in the hospital and awake the following morning only to find an empty bed. When I would inquire about the patient, I was told that they had passed away during the night.

The nurses informed me that the doctor's decision was for me to receive a blood transfusion immediately. I wanted to call my husband but was told that there was no time. When I rebelled against getting the blood transfusion unless I spoke with my husband, I was denied the privilege of using the phone. Determined, I held on to my IV pole and slowly passed the nurses, who also refused to help, and used a public telephone at the end of the hallway. I managed to put the call through to my house, but Cecil had just left for church. I called my tenant upstairs, and with much effort, described what was about to take place. He ran to our church with the message that I was refusing a blood transfusion and I was requesting immediate prayer. Cecil had just finished prayer for our Prayer Album Ministry Segment when he received the note. He called the congregation back to the altar and prayed again.

That afternoon, the choir visited me at the hospital to cheer my spirit with songs of praises to God. Cecil met the doctor in the elevator and inquired of him how the blood transfusion went. To God be the glory, the doctor replied that it had not happened. When Cecil told me about the encounter, I felt something move through my body and knew I had been healed and delivered!

In the midst of all of this, my doctor advised me that he had no choice but to begin dialysis and would place me on the waiting list for a kidney transplant. This list was more than a mile long and I felt that I would not survive the waiting period for this transplant. As the news of my illness spread throughout the churches, the saints everywhere began to pray, seeking God for both healing and deliverance. It lifted my faith in God for me not to accept this terrible diagnosis. I knew that it was possible for me to succumb and die because of the wait, but my life was in God's hands and I was never fearful. One thing I was certain of, that I would live to testify about the healing touch of the Master's hand and that others would definitely be helped by my experience.

I trust in God, I know He cares for me
On mountain bleak or on the rolling sea
Though billows roll, He keeps my soul
My heavenly father watches over me.

Rung 46: Taking Its Toll

I honestly thought this was a setback until I saw the wonder-working power of the blood of Jesus Christ, the Healer. God was really working wonders through the ministry of my husband and me. The enemy became furious and began using some heavy weapons against us. It was evident that he was trying to capture as many souls as he could, but the victory was ours. We knew that we would overcome through Christ.

Three days later, I was dismissed from the hospital, with Dr. DeRose planning to begin the dialysis process. He knew that I was not happy with the thought of dialysis so he gave me an alternative. The medication regime began with sixteen-and-a-half pills per day, including seven egg whites and as much water as I could drink. On this regime I could not miss a dosage or the method would be aborted, and we would be right back at Plan A: Dialysis. I believed that I started the medication right as the illness was beginning to take its toll on my body. Two weeks went by before I felt any better, and my upward progress was a stable and steady one.

After three weeks, I was scheduled for a check-up to see whether my body was responding to the medication. If not, I knew that dialysis would begin immediately. To ensure that my medication was given and taken as prescribed, my husband assigned someone from our church to be with me for as long as was needed. Being confined to my home and my bed with nothing much to occupy my time but prayer, I had no choice but to watch my physical structure blow up before my eyes. I began to have a moon face and buffalo shoulders. Many people who had not seen me for a while could barely recognize me.

The medicine was prescribed for one year and six months. During those days, I could hardly pick my head up from my pillow. Some of the medication caused my skin to blacken, and had terrible side effects such as leaving black blotches on my tongue and arms. With all of this, I was holding onto God's unchanging hand. My foundation was not shaken in the least, even when the enemy tried to generate fear. I must confess though that there were times when I could not pray. Though I could not utter a word verbally, in my heart was a song.

> I've found a friend in Jesus; He's everything to me;
> He's the fairest of ten thousand to my soul;
> The Lily of the Valley, in Him alone I see
> All I need to cleanse and make me fully whole.

In sorrow He's my comfort, in trouble He's my stay;
He tells me every care on Him to roll;

He's the Lily of the Valley,
The Bright and Morning Star;
He's the fairest of ten thousand to my soul.

With everything going on, I tried to be present at every service unless I was out of town. As soon as the doors of the church were opened, I would be there. I was given a special chair so that I could elevate my legs because of the swelling. Though I looked bad, I was feeling better. The enemy took the opportunity to present himself to me every day. He told me often that I would never get my health back and that I was "washed up." He tried hard to destroy my faith by letting me know that I would not amount to anything. In order for the enemy not to contaminate my thoughts, I kept a clear mind. After he said those things to me, I asked God if He had heard what Satan said. In due time, God answered.

In the Bible, Jehoshaphat says, *"Lord, You told me if when evil comes upon me as the sword, judgment or pestilence or famine, if I stand before Your house and in Your presence and cry unto You from my affliction, then You will hear and help."* My prayer became, *"Lord, I am asking You to help me. Let this plan that the enemy has for my life come to naught because I know You are bigger than any problem or situation that may come upon me. Thou art the Great Physician who heals the sick."*

It is always good to remind God of the things that you have discussed with Him. It is not that God has forgotten, but I believe He uses ways for us to stay in touch with Him prayerfully and earnestly. One of the things that I reminded God about was His promise to give me long life, and there was no way that I could live a hearty and normal life being sick. Every time I reminded God of His promise to me, right away I knew that I was healed regardless of what I thought was reality.

Lying in bed one day, a voice spoke to me saying, "I gave you a voice! Use it." This was rather amazing to me! I asked God many times just to make sure the voice I heard was His. As I questioned Him, I remembered one of the key reasons why I came to New York and the whole recording argument came to me all over again. It was some twenty-two years later and I was still not able to carry out my prophetic plan. At this point, I made God and myself a promise that as soon as I was able, I would fulfill the long-awaited vow. Each day came with a new experience. I literally felt God's healing hands anointing my body as I made my way back to recovery and society.

The doctor kept a constant check on my progress. At this time, I became extremely overweight but felt physically well and continued taking the medication. Waiting for my change, I knew that I would not be in this state for any time much longer. The road to recovery was a very long and impatient one. Eighteen months felt like serving a life sentence for a crime I did not commit. Sometimes the "Why me, Lord?" pity party entered my heart, but then I quickly corrected myself with "Why not me?" God allowed the enemy to touch my body, but I had the faith and the confidence that the same God would heal and deliver me.

Dr. DeRose's secretary left a message on our answering machine saying that the doctor needed to see me the next day at ten o'clock in the morning. The call was frightening, yet I knew that it could not be anything much worse. He was only informing me that I needed to be drinking gallons and gallons of water every day, starting on the following Monday. This was because I would need to begin emptying my bladder into a container each night and then take it to the hospital for a protein check. I had to do this for the next two to three months. In addition, I began visiting the hospital every other day to check if the sinews were forming again in my joints. Everything was going in such a positive direction and the hearts of many who had prayed were made glad.

But I still had no strength. Even when I tried to muster up vigor, I failed. Cecil probably thought that I might never regain my original beauty, so I prayed that he would be able deal with these strange features and be patient until I was back to my usual self. During this time, he never allowed me to feel insignificant or unwanted, and I appreciate him a lot because he was in constant prayer for my full recovery.

One day while incapacitated waiting to get well, I guess I must have looked uncomfortable because my brother-in-law who was visiting from Jamaica noticed my sad countenance and, in an assertive tone of voice, told me to stop feeling guilty for being dormant at home. My focus needed to be on getting better; that was the most important thing at that time. He assured me that I would be fine and that one day I would be able to testify to how I overcame.

A year later, I decided that I would drive myself to the nail shop to get a manicure and pedicure. Cecil had gone to work, the children were at school, and my assistant, Rosie, was on her day off. Before leaving, Rosie had set up all my dosages exactly as they were to be taken and made frequent calls to ensure that I followed instructions. Between medications,

I got into the car and drove myself to the nail shop. I was happy because I was able to do something besides lie helplessly in bed.

Halfway into my pedicure, the floor of the shop began moving. It felt like someone had pulled the rug out from under me. The people in the shop looked as though they were spinning around me. The next moment my face was wet. The pedicurist, trying to revive me, had placed a cold rag on my face. In the distance, I could hear someone asking for my information and getting ready to call 911. Finally, somewhat revived, I made a call to Rosie's home, praying that she was there. I thanked God when she answered her telephone, and I explained with difficulty where I was.

In a short time, Rosie was there with a look of amazement and anger. She asked me if I had taken a cab to the shop and was even more surprised when I told her that I had driven. I remembered her telling me that she was able to drive but did not have a driver's license. For us to get the car home without Cecil knowing what had happened, Rosie had to drive. With shaking knees, we got into the car, and with a little tutoring between my unconscious spells, she was able to drive me home and park the car just where Cecil had left it. Rosie spent the rest of her day off scolding me like a child and making me promise her that I would never do that again. The truth behind her speech made me believe that I was probably never going to get back to my normal self.

However, I was determined to push myself into a positive mode and was strong-willed for another try. Two months after my nail shop experience, I decided to go for another drive, feeling that I was ready to tear my hair out if I did not get out of the house. After waiting for Rosie's day off and for my husband to go to work and the children to school, I boldly took the car and went for a drive. While driving, I could have sworn that I saw the road rise up in front of me. I immediately turned the car around and headed back home. The enemy wanted me to believe that I had become disoriented and would be off balance for the rest of my life.

But when the enemy says no, God says yes!

A wonderful Savior is Jesus my Lord
A wonderful Savior to me
He hideth my soul in the cleft of the rock
Where rivers of pleasure I see

A wonderful Savior is Jesus my Lord
He taketh my burden away
He holdeth me up, and I shall not be moved
He giveth me strength as the day

When clothed in His brightness transported I rise
To meet Him in the clouds of the sky
His perfect salvation, His wonderful love
I'll shout with the millions on high

During this trying time I gathered so much strength and courage and received the assurance that I could go up to the next rung. My healing was slow, but I trusted in God. I was determined not to go under but to continue looking forward to tomorrow as a brighter day would dawn.

Though life may be wearing a different face today,
Tomorrow Jesus will turn my night to day.

Rung 47: Jesus Christ, The Healer

*I*t was a Monday morning appointment with Dr. DeRose. I sat in his Bay Ridge office waiting for my name to be called. The prayer in my heart for almost eighteen months was that the medication regime would be terminated. When I went in, he began talking with me about stuff that had nothing to do with my illness – casual conversation was something I was in no mood for.

The nurse came in, checked my vital signs, and directed me to the bathroom for a urine specimen to see if I had any protein spillage. Eagerly, I waited for Dr. DeRose to come out of the testing room where I heard him laughing. I figured that he was getting me in a pleasant mood to break whatever news he had for me. I looked at him as he walked in with a grin on his face as wide as the Atlantic Ocean. He sat down, pushed back in the chair, and told me that I was not only cured, but healed. There was not one trace of protein and my kidneys were functioning fine. I did not know whether I should laugh or cry. I was sitting there, frozen in shock, even though I had somewhat expected good news.

Dr. DeRose informed me that this could not be explained. I had arrived as an almost dead woman over a year ago and now look what had happened. I was cured! He began to congratulate me for taking the medication as prescribed because if I hadn't this would not have been possible. Dr. DeRose is an excellent physician and he bragged about his work. At first, I thought that he was just impudent, but after experiencing his medical attention firsthand, I saw the reason for his confident attitude. His advice was that I continue on half of a small pill for six more weeks just so he would not be too drastic in discontinuing my medication level.

That's when it hit me! I began to laugh like I had lost my mind, and right away I felt strength in my body. I left his office with an appointment to return in six weeks. The doors of the prison I was in opened and I walked out like Paul and Silas. As I drove home, I stopped at a stop-light on Fort Hamilton Parkway and jumped out of the car. I ran around it, hollering, "*I am well! I am healed! Oh, glory to God!*" People looked at me as if I had lost my mind, but they had no idea of what the Lord had done for me.

Passing one of my favorite restaurants on the way home, I pulled over and had a big lunch. After I got home and read the instruction sheet the nurse had given me, I saw that I was supposed to eat only small portions. My food group had not changed; I only had to pay attention with much care. With the extra weight, I had to be extra careful about what I ate. When I asked Dr. DeRose about a diet, he discouraged me and asked me to wait until the medication was out of my system.

I began to testify of the goodness of the Lord and how he had healed me of my kidney disease. My God! I was taken back at some responses; I thought everyone would be jubilant. Instead of rejoicing and celebrating, some people were actually disappointed. This was something that I never thought could exist in Christendom. One associate even asked me to stop testifying about my healing because people were starting to look at me differently. The claim was that my healing was causing some of the congregants to shy away from me. At first, I listened. Then one day, I was causally speaking about my deliverance and God reminded me about where He had brought me from. When God heals you, you should tell others! They may be in the same position you were in and need a word to build their faith and receive their healing. There are many testimonies of God's healing power. Tell it far and wide!

God not only healed me from a kidney disease, He replenished my joints and bones with calcium, which allowed me to walk in the newness of life. I knew that I had gotten a new lease on life. This changed my whole thought pattern and gave me the added encouragement to do whatever was left undone. To experience the healing touch of Jesus' hand is something that I will never forget. Sometimes it takes a setback to have a comeback.

The sickness I experienced opened my eyes to a lot of wickedness in high places. I was being very careful of the people who prayed for me, knowing that there were wolves in sheep's clothing lurking at every corner. The saints of God need to learn to pray for themselves, especially when the Spirit will not release a freedom in their spirit to have someone else pray for them. There are saints who know that they are not in fellowship with the person they are praying for; they just want to make a good show to those around them. They carry out a false prayer, which only wastes our time and goes no further than the ceiling.

I thank God that I know Him for myself. My setback was an evil that was unleashed on me, but I thank God that when no one else was around to help or even give me an assuring smile or a genuine prayer , He was there. Sometimes a word of encouragement can take an individual a long way. I spent long hours talking with Jesus, reminding Him of the reason I came to the United States, and of His promises. He comforted me and I was confident not be afraid, only believe (Mark 5:36).

Who His own self bore our sins in His own body on the tree,
that we, being dead to sin, should live unto righteousness:
by whose stripes ye were healed.
(1 Peter 2:24)

Healing is the children's bread. Sometimes we do not need healing for the physical body, but for the mind and the spirit. The body may be functioning quite well, but the heart can be spiritually wounded.

Just as when someone undergoes an operation, they take a longer time to heal than from a simple incision. I know that I must forgive those who have wounded me. For many, many years I carried some wounds. I was aware of every wrong that was done toward my family and me. Ignoring the situation, I made myself believe that everything was okay. It took me a long time before I addressed it, but by fasting and prayer I overcame. The years were long and the road was rough. Sometimes I felt that I could not go around the bend, or that I would fall over a cliff if I tried. God hid me from the angry, raging seas of life's unfairness, witchcraft, jealousy, envy, malice, stress, and anger. Oh, there were many wounds, but under His wings I found the balm for my healing. Today I can say:

I am free, praise the Lord I'm free
No longer bound, no more chains holding me
My soul is resting, it's such a blessing
Praise the Lord, Hallelujah! I'm free.

An unforgiving spirit is a hindering spirit that has been lingering among the saints. The enemy causes so many things to happen within the fellowship that would give us reason to hold grudges and to be unforgiving. Thanks be to God for the mighty work He has done in me. I have let go of all the hurt. It took a moment – a long moment. There were times when I would be driving alone in my car and discussing my hurt with the Lord. I would cry, laugh, and get angry, even bitter. My caution is. If we have in any way allow hurt to destroy our relationships with our friends or families, or if ever we have caused someone's feet to slip or stumble and were aware of it, find the courage to make amends. In order for us to move to the next level, we need healing and deliverance.

Many times the reason why we are not healed of our infirmity, whether physically, mentally or spiritually, is because we hold animosity in our heart which walks hand in hand with the unfruitful works of darkness. Lack of forgiveness can hide in a place of pain that we haven't allowed God's finger to touch yet. We have blocked the flow of the Spirit of God. I know it is hard, but there is nothing too hard for God. He knows all about our struggles and will guide us. He is ready and able to heal you.

Rung 48: The Accident, Part 1

As my health improved, Cecil suggested that it was time to shop for another house. His aim was to surprise me, so he kept the type of house and location a secret until he was sure. Finally, he took me to see the property. I was indeed pleased with his choice, and certainly the children loved it, too. A few months later, we began moving in, thanking God for His blessings on us.

The house we had lived in on Winthrop Street was not altogether convenient to host the many guests who came from time to time to attend church conventions and conferences. The inconvenience that came when we retired each night caused a little discomfort, but we had managed well.

The move was a major effort. We had lived on Winthrop Street for eighteen years and we all found it very difficult to leave. The thought of moving brought some sadness.

One day, while I was transporting some small appliances to the new house, a U-Haul truck disregarded the red stop light and totaled my car. My driver's side door fell off as the car came to a halt. I heard glass breaking in the distance. I opened my eyes and looked up at the sky, slipping in and out of consciousness. I noticed the ambulance there and the paramedics attending to me. I thank God I sustained only minor injuries: a broken middle finger on my right hand and minor cuts and bruises. A thorough examination was done and four hours later I was released from the hospital emergency room. To God be all the Glory!

What have I to dread, what have I to fear,
Leaning on the everlasting arms
I have blessed peace with my Lord so near
Leaning on the everlasting arms.

Rung 49: Finally

*I*n December of 1994, a team of us went to Jamaica for our annual crusade. We visited a long-standing friend, Mr. Noel Willis, at the office and studio of the "Grace Thrillers," where we were given a tour of the property. Mr. Willis showed us the new studio where his gospel group recorded and offered us a reasonable rate if ever I decided to do any recording. I immediately set plans in motion to take up the challenge as soon as the New Year arrived.

At the beginning of this December, I told one of the parishioners of our church that I would like to record Christmas songs as a project for my contribution to the customary holiday activities. I would record from our church's radio room and the proceeds from the sale would be my contribution. With a good heart, she discouraged me and suggested that I do a proper recording. I was fully convinced now; the Lord was showing me that it was time. Mr. Willis visited us in New York during Easter of 1995 and assured me that it would be worth it to begin the recording process. I knew this was my life-long dream coming true.

It was a few months before the recording when Cecil, under the anointing of the Holy Spirit, preached the sermon, "Coming Back from the Setback." During the sermon I was inspired to write the title song, *From the Setback*, for my debut album,

The sermon dovetailed so well with my life's story that I was inspired to connect the dots. Finally, I was on my way to Jamaica for my first recording session. It took a week to lay the tracks and another few months for the final dot to be connected. God began to bless my singing ministry with my first CD, *From the Setback*.

It is still one of my best-selling CDs. Before Christmas of the next year, another new CD was released, *Christmas at Home, with Eleanor*. The spirit of recording grew more and more favorably every year and I continued to make my dream of singing professionally a reality. Invitations to minister at various concerts, weddings, banquets, and church services began pouring in, with the opportunity to travel the world extensively.

The closer I come to fulfilling my dream, the more opposition presented itself. Satan tried to hold me back with another setback that could have brought much more pain and hurt than I could ever imagine.

Rung 50: The Accident, Part 2

I had just returned from a singing engagement in St. Vincent and the Grenadines, and was spending time with our daughter, Elizabeth. She was telling me about her mini vacation to Jamaica. We were both excited about our trip, and as we drove, we exchanged our experiences with enthusiasm. As we approached the red traffic light, I heard loud tire screeches from behind. Glancing in my rearview mirror, I saw a car approaching with no intention of stopping. Sure enough, the speeding car slammed right into the back of our vehicle and shoved us under the back of the truck in front of us. Shocked and screaming, we watched our car become smaller and smaller as the momentum of the car behind us continued pushing us into the truck. We thought this was the end. Luckily, the driver veered from behind us and hit a tree on the side of the road. A motorist quickly called 911.

An ambulance came and we were taken to Kings County Hospital, where we were checked and kept for observation for a little while. After being treated for minor injuries, we were released and sent home.

May I remind you that your setback is only a set-up for a dynamic, Spirit-filled and anointed comeback?

Chapter 10
WHY I SING

Rung 51: He Gave Me a Song

I've been singing about my Lord for many years
I've sung when I am happy, I've sung when I have tears
And some folks may even question that it's all been just a show
But the reason why I'm singing I want the world to know

I sing because there is an empty grave
I sing because there is that power that saves
I sing because His grace is real to me
I sing because I know I'm not alone
I sing because someday I'm going home
Where I'll sing throughout Eternity.

*T*here is always someone questioning what I do, especially if it is something that is attractive in appearance or value. The question that is asked sometimes when I am being interviewed is "Why do you sing?" This is a good question, as some gospel singers sing because they are gifted, not knowing Jesus Christ as their personal Lord and Savior, with an added anointing. This gives me the opportunity to tell the interviewer about Christ Jesus. I think that gospel artists should know Jesus first, and is happy to identify with Him before singing of Him. Knowing Him gives me a good enough reason why I sing.

It does not matter whether or not we can modulate our voices; this is not an issue. As long as you are able to lift your voice and sing unto the Lord the glory that is due to His Name, that's all that matters. Singing is a language of joy. If you are angry, upset, or cursing at someone, you cannot sing.

On the island of Jamaica, there are areas with a number of building complexes called tenement yards. These complexes are made up of five or six houses built for high occupancy by the government for low-income households. Often enough, the tenants that live in the tenement yard find it hard to get along. During these disagreements, an individual might begin singing. This singing is not to be confused with singing praises unto the Lord. The sole purpose of that song is to imply to the other individual that they are being ignored.

A song is putting your voice in modulation to melodies in waves of different tones. When I gave my heart to Jesus, I was a child. My conscience was geared towards serving Him and singing for Him. I wanted the joyfulness of my youth to stay with me forever through song. When learning a new song, I would spend hours rehearsing, making sure I knew why I sang it and thinking about what the words meant to me. So when I am asked why I sing, in addition to the obvious reason, I am given an opportunity to tell of Jesus and His love.

I honestly believe walls were made for backs. The saying goes, "When my back is against the wall, who I should call on?" Sometimes we are in situations that cause us to look around for God and wonder if He's still there. Usually it takes a song to lift the load and lighten the burden. Let me remind you of a few verses in the book of the Psalms which encourage me to sing.

> *Sing unto the LORD, O ye saints of His,*
> *and give thanks at the remembrance of His holiness.*
> (Psalms 30:4)

> *One thing have I desired of the LORD, that will I seek after;*
> *That I may dwell in the house of the LORD all the days of my life,*
> *to behold the beauty of the LORD, and to inquire in His temple.*

> *And now shall mine head be lifted up above mine enemies round*
> *about me: therefore will I offer in His tabernacle sacrificed of joy;*
> *I will sing, yea, I will sing praises unto the LORD.*
> (Psalms 27:4-6)

> *Sing praises to God, sing praises:*
> *sing praises unto our King, sing praises.*
> *For God is the King of all the earth:*
> *sing ye praises with understanding.*
> (Psalms 47:6-7)

It is very easy for a child of God to get the enemy off his or her back. Sometimes we would say, "I have a monkey on my back." Do not use the clichés that the world often repeats; these useless words cannot help the children of God. Anything that is on our back has to be a burden, and "*burdens are lifted at Calvary; Jesus is very near.*"

As I continue in my singing ministry, I make a special effort to choose songs that will make a difference in our everyday pilgrimage. There is a song to fit every situation life throws at us. My desire is to equip each of us with the perfect songs for those times. If my singing does not help someone, then it is in vain. Many people would prefer to attend a gospel concert rather than listen to a sermon. Nothing can take the place of the anointed Word from an anointed speaker, and likewise, nothing can fill that void of an anointed song like, "*I need thee every hour, most gracious Lord,*" from an anointed singer.

There was a story told of *The Drowning Singer*, who was in a horrible shipwreck. Before he died, the onlookers thronged the beach to watch the devastation, wishing that they had the power to cross the waters to save him. He was clinging to a fragment of the ship's debris without hope but kept afloat while the rest of the ship sank and all who were aboard lost their lives. They tried to send a message to him through a trumpet with words from a sermon they remembered, but they failed. So they shouted through the trumpet, "Look to Jesus! Can you hear?" When they listened for his reply, someone said, "He is singing!"

Jesus lover of my soul,
let me to thy bosom fly,
while the nearer waters roll,
while the tempest still is high!
hide me, oh my savior hide,
till the storm of life is past;
safe into the heaven guide
O receive my soul at last!

The story tells us that the wind brought back the echo and everyone was pleased to hear him singing bravely from the waters, "*Oh, receive my soul at last.*" The singer dropped into the tossing sea, as the watchers, who were looking homeward through tear-filled eyes, said that he passed to be with Jesus with the singing of that hymn.

When my night is upon me and the pressures of life's billows roar, I cling to the Rock. I know Him as the one who calms the storm. It gives me a gratifying feeling when I can reach out during stormy seasons of distress and grief, and find solace, comfort, and peace. That is also one of the reasons why I sing.

When I showed my mother my passport with the stamp from the American Embassy in Kingston that permitted me to visit the United States, through her tears she sang the hymn, "*Jesus, lover of my soul; let me to thy bosom fly.*" This spontaneous hymn soothed her excitement and happiness. She immediately thanked God for His kindness in opening up a new door. As children, we saw that singing was her usual custom of acknowledging God for all He had done.

The songs I write are inspired by personal experience. When I experience joy and happiness, I love to sing a happy song and maybe dance a little to thank God and nestle in His goodness. If my life takes a turn for the worse, the Holy Spirit reminds me that the Bible says that I should give God thanks in all things, and I still sing a song of praise. I want every listener to understand my feelings when I belt out the lyrics of a song. Whether happy or sad, I know that whatever caused me to sing was all allowed by God.

Sometimes before a service officially begins, I bow before God in song and prayer. My heart is made merry when I can share my life in song with my fellow church members and all who are willing to listen. I am glad for that opportunity because I know that someone can benefit from knowing that if I can sing in a time of suffering or pain, so can they. My motto will be: *As long as I live, let me live for others, let me bless others.*

Rung 52: The Beauty of a Song

The trusting heart to Jesus clings,
nor any ill forebodes,
But at the cross of Calv'ry sings,
Praise God for lifted loads!

Singing I go along life's road,
Praising the Lord, praising the Lord
Singing I go along life's road
For Jesus has lifted my load.

There was hardly a time I could remember when there was not a song in my heart. Sometimes, I would catch myself singing a song I hardly knew, just because I wanted to sing. Singing brings freedom to the mind, spirit, soul, and body.

Often God would give me a song to share with the congregation. Even old songs, when sung in the spirit, can bring forth a beauty and turn worship service into a revival. A song can change a sinner of the deepest dye into a saint.

When you have surrendered your life to God, your heart should be filled with songs of praise and adoration to God. New believers are sometimes unable to express their innermost thoughts to God through their own words, but when the words of a song express the feelings they find hard to verbalize, they feel relieved. A believer knows the true worth of a song. Healing virtue can be sent to any infirmity through a song. The bound can be set free through the words and anointing of a song. A song of deliverance, courage, and strength captivates the beauty of Christ and Christian life.

James McGranahan wrote this beautiful song:

Sinners Jesus will receive:
Sound this word of grace to all
Who the heav'nly pathway leaves,
All who linger, all who fall.

Sing it o'er and o'er again:
Christ receiveth sinful men.
Make the message clear and plain:
Christ receiveth sinful men.

I love when a song is full of good news, especially a song that expresses the love of God through salvation. People have always complimented me about the words of the songs I write, and I am always ready to share the gospel of Christ. He is the one worthy of adoration.

Jesus is the source of my lyrical flow. I try to send clear and profound messages that will soothe the weary, cheer the oppressed, and lift the heavy-hearted, but most of all, change the heart of the listener who doesn't believe. The world must know that Jesus still saves.

I fully understand how preachers feel when, through the inspiration of the Holy Spirit; they are able to deliver a sermon that causes one to yield to the tender embrace of the Spirit of God, leaving them thoroughly cleansed from sin.

While visiting friends in Pennsylvania many years ago, we went into a Christian bookstore. While they shopped, I went browsing for songbooks. I found a song that I had not heard in a long while and was overjoyed. My friends could not understand why I had paid so much for a songbook that contained only one song that I was familiar with. I was not only blessed by that one familiar song, but by all the songs. Even though I did not know them all, the words appealed to me. I knew that someday I would be able to learn and sing the songs I didn't know.

Some years later, I heard a song by Dottie Rambo, "*I Will Glory in the Cross*," and sure enough, it was in the book that I had purchased years earlier. Dottie told a story about how she was asked not to sing about the cross of Christ because it was considered gory, and people do not want to hear about the blood or the cross. She did sing that night, "*He looked beyond my fault and saw my need.*" Everyone was weeping, including the man who did not want her to sing about the cross or the blood. Dottie spoke of how that night, back in her hotel room; she had repented of her disobedience of not wanting to sing about the cross, the blood and His grace. As she lay in the dark, the Lord assured her:

I boast not of works, nor tell of good deeds.
For naught have I done to merit His grace.
All glory and praise shall rest upon Him,
So willing to die in my place.

I will glory in the cross, in the cross,
Lest His suffering all be in vain.
I will weep no more for the cross that He bore
I will glory in the cross.
By Lindsay L. Terry

As Christians, we have a mandate on our lives to let the world know how much Jesus suffered for us to live in abundance. Even in song, we can profess how wonderful Christ is and how he gives us beauty for ashes. I have been blessed to share the beauty of Christ in my singing ministry through radio and television, reaching millions across the Eastern Caribbean islands and destroying the yoke of bondage that the enemy has on God's people.

I have heard many testimonies about how various songs have brought individuals through their crises: whether they are sickness, death, or despair. Songs have lifted spirits and strengthened them emotionally, physically, and most importantly, spiritually.

On one occasion, I was ministering through song at a concert, and in the middle of a song, the sound was turned off. I was thinking that something had gone wrong with the electricity until I noticed that the lights were still on in the auditorium. Then I thought that it was my soundtrack, so I looked at the engineer. He was still sitting down, not looking worried or trying to see what the problem was. I finished the song *a cappella*. When I came off the stage, I immediately asked him what had gone wrong. The engineer replied, "Nothing!" In my heart, I knew the devil was trying to stop the Word of God from being heard through my song. I finished my song because I knew that I would glory in the cross no matter what the plan of the enemy was.

People who have not known Jesus Christ as their Savior write some of the greatest songs that I have ever heard. I have often pondered the question: If they were not saved, how were they inspired? Some people believe that to sing a gospel song makes them an undisputed shoe-in for the kingdom of heaven. I am always elated to articulate the blessings that come through a song because I know the One whom I sing about personally.

When I suffered my setback, never once did I rest or forfeit the Christian race. I knew I just had to go on. In my loins were the songs of strength for today and bright hope for tomorrow. I cherished the gift of singing and would do nothing to violate this precious anointing. The Lord kept a melody deep down in my heart and a true message to share because He knew how it would rescue a struggling soul one day.

My sole desire and determination is to spread the gospel of Jesus Christ through my gift of song to a dying world. If I chose to neglect the call of God to sing, I would have to explain on judgment day what I did with the talent He had entrusted to me. Let us not bury our talents, but multiply them and be pleasing before God.

Give of your best to the Master,
give of the strength of your youth.
Throw your soul's fresh, glowing ardor,
into the battle for truth.
Jesus has set the example.
Dauntless was He, young and brave.
Give Him your loyal devotion,
Give Him the best that you have.

Rung 53: Bringing Happiness

*E*very time I begin a recording, I get a sudden burst of energy, a wonderful sensation that I'm flying high, feeling no pain. I love when I walk into a recording studio knowing that God has recruited me to help to make Him and His love famous. He has delivered me from so much and has spoken to me so many times and knows that I am one of the best advertisements for the Great Confederation of Brotherhood – Christianity.

After four recordings, I decided to excel and take my singing ministry to another level. With that in mind, I registered for a weekend of workshops at the Gospel Academy of Music Arts in Nashville, Tennessee.

I was in search of something new, a different sound to Eleanor Riley's music. The workshops I participated in were indeed interesting and helpful. In one workshop, we had to allow our songs to be critiqued. The suggestions I received stimulated changes that reflected the exact newness I wanted. I was happy I traveled to Nashville, even if it was only because of the insight I received. I also had the privilege of meeting with other gospel artists who were determined to assist me in any way possible to carry out the new ideas I received in the enhancement workshops.

In between breaks, I wandered around the different booths, curious as to what they were all about. I came upon a booth advertising a producer, songwriter, and motivational speaker with giveaways and other paraphernalia. I took a business card that he offered.

Upon returning to Brooklyn, I had a feeling, even before I contacted the producer to discuss my intentions, that this business card would lead me to new accomplishments. It was as if the recording was already done, so the joy I felt was one of fulfillment.

That business card was for Eric Copeland, who at the time resided in Kentucky. After I contacted him, he was very excited and confessed that if he had gone to the music workshop just to meet me it would have been worth his time and effort. We spent quite a while setting up dates for consultation and studio work. Shortly after, I was on my way to Kentucky to record my fifth album, *My Story*. The sessions went well and we worked together as if we had known each other for years. Eric's wife was also instrumental in this recording and it was her suggestion to name the album *My Story*.

The many flights to Kentucky were not cheap, but they were worth every dime when I heard the beautiful songs on the album. The musical ability of Eric, who is American-born and raised, was that of a West Indian-born reggae producer. Many have asked me which part of Jamaica Eric came from and were flabbergasted when I replied that he was not only American but was also white! So I made him an honorary citizen of Jamaica.

In July of same year, 2002, I launched my new album at my home church, Freedom Hall Church of God in Brooklyn, New York. The evening was filled with excitement and praises. Several gospel artists shared the stage with me as the Spirit of God filled the air. The launch was done in several locations across the world.

I am always working on a new project. As I launch a new album, I'm getting another one ready. Eric would always inquire of the new CD, the marketing accomplishments, and distributions. He encouraged me to go for another recording after one year. That was always a sweet tune to my ear as this was my life. I remembered the years that I had spent waiting for the opportunity and was determined to make good use of it. God has been faithful to me in blessings and in providing the funds from these previous projects to finance the new ones.

A year later, I was back in the studio laying down rough tracks for my sixth album, *From My Heart.* The rough work was done in Nashville, Tennessee, where Eric was spending a few weeks producing other projects. The times of recording were always rough and strenuous. Fitting the schedule of studio work into traveling to various singing engagements, church conventions, and crusades was tedious.

Since I had been blessed and had so much fun doing this, I asked a question of the Lord: "Why was I really hindered in the first place?" Before He answered me, the reasons popped up one after the other in my mind. One reason stood out more than the rest. The delay came because of my babies – I would not have been able to do studio work while they were young. It would have been too hard. I thanked God more than ever for showing me His way and not mine.

At the conclusion of the great recording, *From My Heart,* the Lord led me to a high school auditorium in Brooklyn where I arranged a launching extravaganza that included other famous gospel artists. It was scheduled for January of 2003.

The auditorium was packed to capacity as the songs were sung under the anointing of the Holy Spirit. Dignitaries from all over were in attendance and enjoyed the evening. The songs ministered in a very personal and sobering way, meeting everyone at the point of their need. The CD rose to the number one position on the Caribbean radio chart for many months, thus giving me opportunities for concerts on other religious occasions to present the album far and wide, mainly in the Caribbean islands. This CD is the most requested album and has been a tremendous blessing everywhere it is aired. Thanks be to God for His blessings.

I was the perfect picture of happiness as the doors continued to open, financially. As gospel music spreads across the world, the blessing of the Lord catches me and overtakes me. Today, I continue to write, sing, and record.

During a recording break, my producer and his family relocated to Nashville, Tennessee, under the direction of the Holy Spirit. The Lord broadened his horizons in the gospel music industry and gave him more clients than he could sometimes handle. This was an answer to his prayer, and I rejoiced with him.

In January of 2005, I headed to Nashville again to do work on my seventh album, *Goodness and Mercy.* This special project had live music played by one of the best bands in Nashville. The band was extra special because all the members were born-again Christians. They knew who they were in Christ Jesus, and played skillfully. This CD is outstanding in so many ways and has ministered to thousands who have heard it. Among the songs recorded is one of my own compositions.

Some say He is my rock in a weary land
Some say He keeps my feet from shifting sand
He's my shelter from the storm
To my tempest brings a calm
Whatever He may be
He brings safe harbor to me.

Oh, He is my safe harbor
He is my safe harbor
He is my refuge and my fortress
My strength in times of weakness
His hand of mercy stills the waves
He is my safe harbor.

Sometimes when troubles rise I see His face
Sometimes in helplessness I look for grace
My hope in Christ will never fail
He's standing in the vale
Rock of Ages cleft for me
I find safe harbor in thee.

The singing experience took me through some rough rungs – some I barely could climb and others that took me near to death, but I made it. If nothing else brings a blessing to me during my Christian journey, just to have the assurance that I am safe and secure from all alarms is of priceless value to me.

Many times I felt worn out, alone, despised, and forsaken, but I have a song in the night. Friends may have gone, but to me He is a friend to the friendless. I found a precious friend; His name is Jesus.

I was listening to the testimonies of the saints during one of our Sunday night services and everybody was saying who Jesus was to them. I was thinking to myself that Jesus is my shelter from the storms. When the rains came, He hid me in His shadow. My vessel has run aground many times but He who is the Captain of my ship delivered me out of deep waters. He took me from the shoreline where I was encountering too many dead things, and too much garbage, and I waded out into the deep because the deep was calling me. Hallelujah!

Did you know that the deeper the waters, the calmer the waves? I was suffering from too many beatings from the waves, so He helped me. God is my safe harbor.

Rung 54: Goodness and Mercy Follow Me

Goodness and Mercy gained the attention of many. This title song of my seventh CD, *The Psalm of David*, was presented to the public in October of 2005 in a gigantic concert which lasted four hours. Hearts were blessed, spirits were lifted, and souls revived.

This CD was well received on the airways and everywhere it was aired. Reviews of this album, along with previous ones, appeared in popular newspapers and magazines across the United States.

I am fully persuaded that the Lord is not over and done with me yet. There are many more songs to be written, sung, and recorded. Every time I receive a prophetic word about my latter years being better than the former, the Holy Spirit confirms it.

I have the witness that the Lord has quite a bit in store for me. The level that He is about to take me to will dumbfound the enemy. I have higher rungs to climb before reaching that final one.

When David personalized 23rd Psalm, he was showing off how good our Lord is. He was lifting up the God he served, reminding himself that no matter what he goes through, he will not fear, because God is well able.

If you noticed, all the way from the beginning to "the setback," the Lord was with me and still hasn't left my side. He indeed brought me through many dangers and around so many difficult curves. God permitted them to prove that He is quite capable of protecting me on this journey.

He knew the paths that I had to take better than I did. Impending danger may be up ahead, but the all-sufficient road-map maker is always ready to clear every danger and peril that lurks.

I sing the 23rd Psalm to the tune of an old school hymn I learned as a child: "Goodness and mercy all my life shall surely follow me, and in God's house forever more my dwelling place shall be." This is easier for me to remember every time I am engaged in singing this great song. Please sing it, too.

A songwriter's suggestion:

When you walk through a storm
hold your head up high
and don't be afraid of the dark.

This song is right in line with the following Scripture:

Thou shalt not be afraid for the terror by night;
nor for the arrow that flieth by day;
Nor for the pestilence that walketh in darkness;
nor for the destruction that wasteth at noonday.
(Psalms 91:5-6)

I was participating in a concert sometime ago when the odds were very much against me, but I was unperturbed, God had my back. When I entered the stage, I was like a boxer in the ring. The first rung was very intense. My opponent, the devil, was ready to pull the rug out from under me, but I gave him a knockout punch.

Let destruction come upon him at unawares
and let his net that he hath hid catch himself.
Into that very destruction let him fall.
(Psalms 35:8)

Then God spoke to me in the following way:

I am the LORD thy God, which brought thee out of the
land of Egypt: open thy mouth wide, and I will fill it.
(Psalms 81:10)

I belted out the songs of Zion in the most unusual way under the anointing of the Holy Spirit and watched the devil turn tail and run. The altar was flooded with bawling sinners coming to the cross. However, none of the pastors showed up to help. It was as if they were not familiar with the charged atmosphere and were afraid. The Lord God spoke to me, "Be not afraid because I am with thee." He further spoke that He himself was more than those that were against me. To God be the glory! Many souls were both reborn and reclaimed for the Kingdom, and the believers were strengthened.

The next morning, I visited a church in the community and was asked to minister in song. God anointed my voice to impart some of the songs, and just as the night before, the testimonies warmed the sanctuary, spreading around the community the awesome power of God. It was a welcome breath of fresh air to the ear. Many assured me that they were praying for my continued success; to God be the glory.

Later that night I was again asked to partake in song at another service, and the testimonies were the same. Believers spoke of the blessings they had received, making mention of the power that was manifested the night before. All of this is because of His goodness and mercy; allow it to follow you.

That Man of Calvary, has won my heart from me,
and died to set me free, blessed Man of Calvary.

With all of my heart I can say that I love Him because He has taken all of my sin and let the Holy Spirit come in. When I was lost in sin, without hope, He called my name. He did not call me by the name of Eleanor; he called me by the name Lazarus. He spoke the words, *"Loose her, and let her go."*

As a child, when I accepted Christ, I knew that there was something specific that He wanted me to do. I knew that He was not just calling me to remain at the saving station all the days of my life. There was a story in me to tell to the nations. My prayer is for all those who carry the gospel whether by preaching, in testimony, or in song. Make sure that you have one motive – to lift up Jesus. If you are not lifting up Jesus, repent now, while you have time. There is still room at the cross. Do not be a hypocrite! You are not fooling anyone, certainly not God. You are bartering your hope for eternity and losing it for a moment of joy, the glitter of sin, and the things that it will win. Have you counted the cost?

Sing because you are saved through the blood of Jesus Christ – the same blood that reaches to the highest mountain and flows to the lowest valley, the same blood will turn your life around, and the same blood will wash you white as snow. We are living in the last days, when we need Jesus to be our safe retreat. It is not about who ministers the longest or the loudest.

You need to be divine and devout, changed from the inside out, making yourself ready for His pure service.

I therefore, a prisoner of the Lord, beseech you that ye walk worthy of the vocation wherewith ye are called, with all lowliness and meekness, with longsuffering, forbearing one another in love, Endeavoring to keep the unity of the Spirit in the bond of peace. There is one body, and one spirit, even as ye are called in one hope of your calling; One Lord, one faith, one baptism. One God and one Father of all, who is above all, and through all, and in you all. But unto every one of us is given grace according to the measure of the gift of Christ. Wherefore he saith, when He ascended up on high, he led captivity captive, and gave gifts unto men. (Now that He ascended, what is it but that he also descended first into the lower parts of the earth? He that descended is the same also that ascended up far above all heavens, that he might fill all things.) And He gave some to be apostles; and some, prophets; and some evangelists; and some pastors and teachers; for the perfecting of the saints, or the work of the ministry, for the edifying of the body of Christ: Till we all in the unity of the faith, and of the knowledge of the Son of God, unto a perfect man, unto the measure of the stature of the fullness of Christ.
(Ephesians 4:1-13)

Goodness and mercy will not follow you if you go against the Word of God. You are instruments of His peace, forbearing one another in love, and endeavoring to keep the unity of the Spirit in the bond of peace.

Chapter 11
CONGRATULATIONS

Rung 55: Congratulations are in Order

At the very inception of this book, fear took hold of my thoughts and my memory. I am cognizant of the fact that not everything is recorded. Some things I willfully left out, and some I honestly do not remember. God, who directed me through the mouths of two witnesses, allowed me to write what He wanted me to say. Those things not mentioned really do not matter now. To God be the glory! There may be someone who knows me from childhood and knows some things that should be included in my book and were not. To those I say, if you are reading the paragraph to which your memory connects, just insert what I have omitted and move on. The privilege is yours.

God turned around what the enemy meant for evil, for my good. I am glad I am not history. Every year we commemorate Memorial Day as one big happy family, celebrating life, rejoicing together in peace and love. As a family we have encountered many incidents, situations, even accidents.

Our marriage could have ended in divorce, unfortunately as many others have, but by the grace of God we are almost celebrating thirty years together. The enemy thought He had us, but as Jamaicans would say, "A *fool, you.*" This is a bit of Jamaican patois.

I have been in situations, where I could see myself finishing in a mental institution, but I stood on the promises of God and He kept me. His promise to me is, "I will have you live to experience "Me, God" canceling the negative vibrations approaching me from the enemy." And bless God, when I could not see them, He allowed me to smell them with my spiritual nostrils.

I give thanks to God Almighty for guidance, wisdom, knowledge, and understanding. It is of a truth; you can become anything you want to be.

Sometimes we feel like life has left us in the hands of evil imposters – people who claim to be close to us but in the end we realize that they are really our enemies. They have a hidden agenda. I will remain faithful to my dream and keep my mouth shut until the secrets cannot be damned by anyone. Like Cinderella and the golden slipper, the proof will be in the pudding. Each rung gets me higher and higher.

Chapter 12

SWEET REWARDS

Rung 56: It Was Worth It

And, behold, I come quickly; and my reward is with me,
to give every man according as his work shall be.
(Revelation 22:12)

I have been the First Lady of a dynamic and growing church for the past twenty-five years, and I am still loving it. It is not my shoes that make me who I am, but the Christ who lives within me. This body in which I live has experienced much adversity. From the peripheral, one may only see the glamour, and not understand what it takes to fill my shoes. To be a pastor's wife, I assure you, is a pricey position. Many might say, "Oh, please!" but no matter how much they think they know my husband or me, there is a difference looking in from the outside.

I was a bit apprehensive about the transition to First Lady and some have even suggested that I need to start acting like one! In the first place, I was not married to a pastor. For me to start behaving like a pastor's wife was an idea that I really detested. I am a lady first, and one of my traits that Cecil fell in love with was my lady-like demeanor. Despite the many challenges, the various philosophies, and people's concepts of me, their judgments were never an estimation of who I actually am. No matter what!

But I'd like to take you to my place of sweet rewards. Having matured sufficiently over the years, I am no longer bothered by what people have to say, whether positive or negative. I am like a bottle of old wine, well-fermented. Nothing can change me now. I'm set. Before my transition I had a fearful nature, I wanted to please the whole community. So I was erroneously tagged as naive. The carnivorous spirit of some people caused me to distant myself even from those that meant me well. I was afraid then, but not anymore.

God took care of me without me having to say a word. He fought the battles and I got the victory! The key is not to retaliate. I just thank God for the capacity in which I serve. I pamper myself with a cup of tea, and I am refreshed for the next rung. Those that hurt and need my shoulders, I make myself available. Sometimes I squelch the desire to say, "I am busy", but the intent of my heart is to please God and to maintain my integrity. It's worth it.

My suggestion is "use hospitality one to another without grudging" (1Peter 4:9) and this will give us a feeling of great reward. Pastor's wives, all wives, single women, young and old, enjoy this side of heaven. Every rung of the ladder gives a new anticipation. But God will take it from there. I say all that to say,

> *It pays to serve the Lord in truth*
> *And be faithful to Him and trust Him more*
> *Your reward will be greater than you think,*
> *For God has a plan, that settles within.*

I honestly believe that God stayed His coming for me to enjoy some of my earthly labor, and there is absolutely nothing wrong with that. What I am receiving now is rich, full, and mouth-watering. I remember when times were harder. I used to clean the church with one other person. Now the Lord rewards me with good help so that I can go home and have a cup of my favorite tea.

He has rewarded us with good cooks. My husband prefers my cooking, but if I am incapacitated for whatever the reason, I am still favored.

I used to come home from work on a Friday evening, prepare dinner, and hurry to attend the young people's meeting. At the end of the service, I would hurry home and do chores all night. Again, God rewarded me with super help so that I can do something less taxing.

We spent years sleeping on the floor in order to accommodate missionaries. God has blessed us with a more convenient and spacious home for our family and the mission field delegation.

My gratitude and love goes out to all who have made our lives and load a lot easier. This is an earthly reward that I have gotten used to and would not change it for the world. Thank you so much, especially to my Freedom Hall family.

The joy is mine to serve as First Lady and to function in the capacity for which I am called. My music ministry took a beautiful turn for greater things to come, and because of this I am called away quite often. Eleanor Riley Music Ministry was birthed out of the Freedom Hall Church of God under the leadership of my husband Bishop Dr. Cecil G. Riley. The reward of this ministry is overwhelming, and God continues to open doors for us, one after the other.

I continue to embrace this beautiful opportunity, in which God took time to mold me for His people to work with and enjoy. I thank Him for all the provisions that He has made for my life. Jesus promised me a better home. He has gone to prepare it, and soon He will return to take me there. Enjoying many years of the goodness of the Lord, His love, His promises, His healing, His deliverance, and His keeping care from the onslaught of the enemy, I can say that I like the Christian life. Many think that the enemy comes with a long fork and long tail jacket, but this is not true. He uses whom He will, if you are careless. There may be songs and scriptures repeated during the writing of this book, that I would like to change, but God says no, "that's the way I inspire you, that's how I wanted it to be."

Did you enjoy your tea? I bet that you had more than one cup. I appreciate you taking this tea break out of your busy schedule to know who I am and where I came from. This book is a victory testimony: "*I shall not die but live to declare the works of the Lord. Amen!*" I went to the Word of God and found the courage for the remainder of my voyage, as He replaces the rungs and puts pep into my steps.

Please sing along with me another time:

Each step I take my Saviour goes before me
And with His loving hands He leads the way
And with each breath I whisper, "I adore Thee"
Oh, what joy to walk with Him each day!

Each step I take I know that he will guide me
To higher ground He ever leads me on.
Until some day the last step will be taken,
Each step I take just leads me closer home.

I trust that the material in this memoir will help to develop stalwart saints for the Kingdom, good family patterns, and great Christian ethics.

Life is not a rehearsal. Let each day we live be with the consciousness of the Holy Spirit. So, whichever rung you may be standing on, please watch your step.

One Love,

Eleanor

AUTHOR BIO

*E*leanor Marjorie Riley, the second of nine children, hails from Westmoreland, Jamaica West Indies. She has been married to Bishop Dr. Cecil George Riley for 30 years, and is the mother of two daughters Elizabeth and Esther.

As a child, Eleanor enjoyed the benefit of a spiritual, nurturing environment, surrendering her life to Christ at the early age of 10 years. Her Spiritual Renaissance occurred at the Church of the First Born Clarendon, Jamaica West Indies, when Eleanor sang in Sunday school, children's choirs, and adult choirs, singing occasional solos. In 1970, Eleanor migrated to the USA, where she has continued singing for the Lord.

For the past 25 years, she has been very active in the Freedom Hall Church of God, Inc., ministry where she currently serves as evangelist, choir director, youth director, and soloist along with her other duties as First Lady.

Eleanor has continued to sing internationally through the USA, Canada, and the Caribbean, going on various crusades with her husband, singing before he brings the Word.

After several years of a fruitful music ministry, Eleanor recorded her debut album, *"From the Setback."* She then released *"Christmas at Home with Eleanor Riley," "Taste the Victory," "Flying Higher (Than I've Ever Been)," "My Story," "From My Heart,"* and her latest CD *"Goodness and Mercy."*

A Presentation of
Eleanor Riley Music Ministry

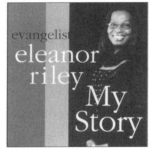
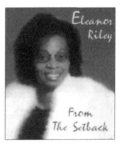

Contact the author at:

Email: Erileystbk@aol.com

Phone: 718-434-7427 or 917-864-0299.

www.creativesoulrecords.com/eleanor

www.cornerstonepublishing.com